THE COMPLETE BLENDER COOKBOOK

A No-Nonsense
Approach
to Successful
Blending

by Zenja Cary
Virginia T. Habeeb

A Benjamin Company/Rutledge Book

Zenja Cary, a specialist in the preparation of food for photography, creates and tests recipes for use in every medium. Her creations have appeared in magazines, including the "Great Dinners" series for LIFE; television; cookbooks; and feature films, including *John and Mary, Diary of a Mad Housewife, Goodbye, Columbus, The Exorcist, Annie Hall,* and *The Wiz.* For the past seventeen years, she has owned her own business, Cary Kitchens, in New York City.

Virginia T. Habeeb was food and home equipment editor of *The American Home* magazine for fifteen years and starred on her own television show, "Virginia's Home Journal." She is director of her own business, Editorial Services, in New York City. A consumer advocate, she is chairman of the Major Appliance Consumer Action Panel (MACAP) and is the author of numerous consumer publications on food and home management. Her books include *Thousands of Creative Kitchen Ideas, The Ladies' Home Journal Art of Homemaking, The American Home All-Purpose Cookbook, The Learn to Cook Book,* and *The MACAP Handbook for the Informed Consumer*. Mrs. Habeeb contributes articles periodically to several major magazines.

ISBN 0-87502-059-3
      0-87502-060-7 pbk.

Published by The Benjamin Company, Inc.
485 Madison Avenue, New York, N.Y. 10022
Prepared and produced by Rutledge Books, Inc.
25 West 43 Street, New York, N.Y. 10036

Library of Congress Catalog Card Number 78-52133
Printed in the United States of America
First printing 1978

CONTENTS

Dear Reader:

A blender is one of the most practical small appliances in your kitchen. The more you use it the more you'll come to appreciate it, to literally depend upon it as one of the best ways to accomplish most food preparation tasks.

The blender is a primary food preparation appliance, important to basic cooking functions. If it doesn't already occupy a prominent place on your kitchen counter, chances are you'll want to make certain it does so from now on.

With a blender at your fingertips and this cookbook on the shelf you will experience new, exciting adventures in cookery —from plain to gourmet! *The Complete Blender Cookbook* is an all-purpose cookbook that contains over 300 recipes, developed in our test kitchens by professional home economists. It differs in only one respect from all other basic cookbooks in that the *blender* itself plays an important role in the preparation of many of the *basic* ingredients in the recipes. And these recipes themselves use the *blender* to its fullest advantage.

4   Perhaps equally important as enjoying the adventure of cookery is developing a working knowledge of basic nutrition and family health. This cookbook offers a wealthy share of nutritional information, as well as tips on cooking and eating for good health.

Improved cooking techniques, changing life-styles, and a growing interest in natural foods and "from scratch" cooking have given the blender a new prominence among kitchen appliances, as part of a basic wardrobe of kitchen electrics so necessary to convenient, economical, and fast food preparation.

So if you have known a blender only by the drinks you mix or the sauces you make, get ready for an amazing discovery. This versatile appliance will perform many common kitchen tasks with amazing speed and efficiency. What you used to think of as chores can now be adventures—and speedy adventures at that.

We promise that you will not only learn to use the blender by following the recipes in this book, but you will develop new cooking techniques, new ways of cooking you never thought possible.

The key to enjoying a blender is to use it frequently. Team it with your other small appliances you have come to depend upon in your everyday cooking techniques. Develop the habit of looking for the steps in a recipe that can be accomplished with the blender. Then it will become second nature to you to reach for this multispeed, miltipurpose appliance.

The rewards you'll reap are limited only by your imagination. Bon appétit!

Hamilton Beach

An Introduction to Blender Cookery

If you have been using a blender, you are familiar with its many abilities. If you are trying one for the first time, get to know what it's all about before you begin using it.

Read the instruction manual *carefully* and *thoughtfully*. Then get started immediately. Prepare a sample recipe—a beverage or a soup or a spread, for example. Practice turning the blender on and off. Experiment with the speeds. Listen to each one. Become familiar with how the motor sounds; how it works; how the blender accomplishes its many tasks. It is a precision instrument that, if handled properly, will produce many exciting results. As you experiment with your blender and the recipes in this book, you will discover many easy shortcuts and speed-ups for everyday cooking tasks.

Begin by using the blender for the simplest kitchen tasks. Grate some cheese for a special casserole. Chop some nuts for a favorite cookie recipe. Make some cracker crumbs for a crunchy pie crust. Study your own recipes to determine which steps the blender can perform for you. Gradually you'll come to depend upon it completely to short-cut many of your food preparation tasks. Keep in mind that when there is a *blending, whipping, stirring, pureeing, beating, crumbing, chopping, grating, mincing, mixing, liquefying, aerating, powdering,* or *churning* task to be done, your blender can do it!

Soon you'll graduate to making your own mayonnaise and producing a foolproof Hollandaise sauce!

General Cooking Terms

To help apply blender cookery to your everyday food preparation, consider the cooking terms you hear daily. Here are some of the most familiar ones and what they mean. You'll recognize them in many of the recipes you make most often. They are common "by hand" food preparation terms that most often refer to the use of special utensils—a knife, a beater, a mixer, a grater, etc. It is amazing how many of these tasks can be performed by the blender and completed more quickly and efficiently:

Beat: To mix with a vigorous, steady motion by hand with a spoon, rotary beater, or wire whisk.

Blend: To mix by hand with a spoon, fork, or wire whisk.

Chop: To cut into relatively small pieces with a knife.

Crush: To mash with a rolling pin, mortar, or other utensil until food is granular, powdered, or pastelike.

Grate: To rub on a grater to produce fine particles.

Grind: To cut into very small particles by putting through a food grinder.

Mince: To chop very fine with a knife.

Puree: To reduce to the consistency of mush by forcing through a fine sieve or food mill.

Stir: To mix gently by hand with a spoon with a rotary motion.

Whip: To beat rapidly by hand, rotary beater, or electric mixer with a vigorous, steady motion.

Look for these terms in familiar recipes and in any new ones you plan to try and then adapt them for blender use.

What a Blender Can Do

Your blender is an all-purpose unit. Think of it as several utensils all rolled up into one appliance. It is in some instances a knife, a grater, a sieve, and a food mill. What you used to think of as time-consuming chores are suddenly quickie jobs done at the flick of a switch.

When you need grated cheese,

When a recipe calls for cracker crumbs,

When you want pureed peas,

When a recipe calls for chopped nuts,

When you want freshly ground coffee,

When you want to blend a Hollandaise sauce,

You can USE YOUR BLENDER!

As you do, you'll find yourself changing your cooking habits with every recipe. Many of the kitchen utensils you normally use for these tasks, such as a grater, a beater, a rolling pin, a food mill, a knife, a grinder, and even a mixer in some cases, will be left on your kitchen shelf.

What a Blender Cannot Do

As you read this book and discover many new recipes and cooking shortcuts, you may begin to think the blender can do everything. But it has some limitations. It is important to know them. There are some tasks that are better done with another appliance.

What a blender does do, it does extremely well. And even what it does not do, it doesn't do badly. However, there are other products that, when teamed with your blender, will accomplish those tasks even better, in addition to performing many other specialized functions. That's why the blender on your counter should be considered only part of a basic wardrobe of the kitchen electrics that will short-cut all food preparation tasks.

As for what the blender itself won't do well, it will not:

Beat egg whites stiff. The blender's great speed breaks down the tender foam as fast as it builds up. Whole eggs and egg yolks, however, may be beaten with other ingredients or alone for scrambled eggs, omelets, and similar recipes.

Mash freshly boiled potatoes. The fast beating action of the blades brings out the starch of the potatoes. Freshly cooked potatoes, however, may be pureed for a blender soup; raw potatoes grated for potato pancakes; packaged instant mashed potatoes improved by blender preparation (see chart, page 14).

Puree the stringy parts of vegetables, such as asparagus stalks or the little sharp spikes that may get into a puree of artichokes.

Grind raw meats or fish. But the blender will chop them for certain recipes and, of course, process cooked meats, poultry, and fish (see chart, page 14).

Knead or mix heavy, stiff doughs. Light doughs are possible (see the bread chapter, page 131).

Extract juice from fruits or vegetables. The blender will liquefy them, however, with the addition of water or other liquid.

Crush ice cubes. The blender container is shaped to process food, not to crush ice cubes. You can liquefy them, however (see chart, page 14).

Whip cream. The blender will not make whipped cream as you know whipped cream. There is not enough area in the container to get enough air into cream to whip it. What the blender does do is beat cream until thickened and slightly increased in volume (see chart, page 14). Cream may also be beaten in with other ingredients.

The Blender Machine

There are basic kitchen appliances, such as electric can openers, knives, and meat grinders, that perform specialized tasks.

In addition, there are food *preparation* appliances, necessary in the processing of food. These include appliances such as food processors, mixers, and blenders. In this book, however, we are concerned only with the blender.

What a Typical Blender Looks Like

Two-Piece Cover
- Tight-sealing cover; odor- and oil-resistant.
- Removable center cap, also a measuring cup, allows easy addition of ingredients while blender is in operation.

Container
- Graduated for easy measuring.
- Clear—constructed of either glass or shatterproof plastic; easy-to-view blender action.
- Open at both ends; spout end provides easy pouring of liquid mixtures; wide enough for removal of nonpouring mixtures.

Gasket
- Provides tight seal; prevents leakage.

Cutting Blade Unit
- Retaining ring.
- Sharp, stainless steel, rust-proof blades; easily removable for thorough cleaning; versatility for use with specially designed jars.

Blender Base
- Powerful motor enclosed in housing of thermoplastic.

Multi-Speed Control Panel
- Provides selection of correct speed plus better control of blender operation. Easy on/off action.

9

The Safety Considerations

Common sense is a basic byword in the operation of a blender or any other small appliance.

1. Read your instruction manual carefully.
2. Keep your hands as well as spatulas and similar utensils away from moving blades.
3. Handle sharp blades carefully.
4. Avoid placing the cutting-blade unit on the base without having the container properly attached.
5. Unplug the cord from the outlet when blender is not in use, before putting on or taking off parts, and always before cleaning.
6. Repair a damaged blender or cord. Return your blender to the nearest authorized service facility for examination, repair, or electrical or mechanical adjustment. Never operate a blender in damaged condition.
7. Do not use any attachments, including canning jars, not recommended by the manufacturer. If you do, please be sure to exercise every precaution. Follow exact instructions to avoid breaking or shattering.
8. Do not immerse base or motor in water or other liquid.
9. Do not use a blender for other than intended use.
10. Keep these instructions.

To Clean a Blender

Quality blender parts are usually corrosion-resistant, hygienic, and easy to clean.

In addition to any special pointers covered in your "Care and Use Manual," follow these simple directions for the care and cleaning of your blender.

Before you clean any section of your blender, *always remember to unplug the cord*.

To Clean Base

- Wipe blender base and cord with a damp cloth or sponge or use a spray-type glass cleaner and wipe dry with a soft towel. To remove stubborn spots, use a mild, nonabrasive cleaner.

To Clean Container

- Unscrew retaining ring and remove it from container.
- Pull out cutting blades from bottom of container.
- Wash retaining ring, gasket, blades, and cover in hot sudsy water; rinse thoroughly and dry. Avoid soaking for long periods of time.
- Wash glass and dishwasher-safe plastic containers in the dishwasher or in hot sudsy water, rinse, and dry thoroughly. Before doing so, however, check your *own* "Care and Use Manual" to make sure the container of your brand is dishwasher-safe.

Always remove cutting assembly (retaining ring, blades, and gasket) after each use and wash and rinse in hot water. Dry thoroughly before putting it away. Rinsing the container with cutting assembly attached is *not* adequate, as "sugary" or "oily" substances such as orange juice and mayonnaise or sauces may accumulate and eventually damage or impair the efficiency of the motor.

11

Another Easy Method to Clean a Blender Container

- Fill container with 2 to 3 cups of warm water and add detergent; cover.
- Turn blender on low speed for a few seconds.
- Remove container from base, rinse, and dry thoroughly.
- Then remove cutting blade unit; wash and dry separately.
- Reassemble.

To Clean Blender Plus® or Other Supplied Additional Containers

- Wash in hot sudsy water, rinse, and dry thoroughly.
- Or wash dishwasher-safe containers and covers in the dishwasher.
- Wash gaskets by hand.

Maintenance

- The motor of your blender is permanently lubricated and will require no oiling. Do not oil.

To Keep Your Blender New-Looking

- Never use scouring pads, harsh detergents, or scouring cleanser to clean container.
- Never place cover or measuring cap in dishwasher.
- Never immerse blender base in water.
- Although the container may be made of either glass or plastic that will not retain odors, it is a good idea to leave the cover off until next use.

The Blending Technique

Some Commonsense Talk about Blender Speeds

The blender is a high-speed motor-driven appliance with an on/off mechanism. Though less expensive blenders have as few as two speeds—low and high—most blenders have a range of at least three speeds—low, medium, and high. The most expensive blenders may have as many as sixteen or more speeds. Whichever model you own, it's the features designed into it that make it different—*more* or *less* convenient to use and *more* or *less* expensive to buy. Some models come with instant on/off controls designed to facilitate short chopping tasks and to prevent overblending. There are also models that come with blend-and-store jars designed for special tasks, such as the preparation of baby foods, relishes, and ground coffee. The newest blender on the market utilizes micro-processor "computer-on-a-chip" technology as its control. This blender performs all basic blending functions plus allows the user to program both blending speed and time at the touch of a finger. Its micro-processor also instantly converts English to metric and vice versa in a variety of cooking-necessary measurements, such as milliliters to teaspoons, grams to ounces, kilos to pounds, etc. Its smooth touch-control surface wipes clean in an instant.

On most blenders, there are many speeds between the lowest speed and the highest speed, which can accomplish various food preparation tasks. These speeds usually are referred to by names such as *stir, whip, puree, crumb, grind, shred, chop, grate, mince, mix, blend,* and *liquefy.* It is important to remember that regardless of the name used for a certain speed, it is the number of that speed that governs what tasks the speed will accomplish.

Not all terms on blenders refer consistently to the same numbered speed. For this reason, we have condensed the numbered speed ranges of blenders into a general "use guide" of low, medium, and high. The chart below describes where various tasks fall within the low, medium, and high speed ranges.

Use this chart to pick the right speed on your blender when preparing the recipes in this book.

Speed Comparison Chart

Whip	1	
Stir	2	
Puree	3	LOW
Beat	4	
Aerate	5	

Crumb	6	
Chop	7	
Mince	8	MEDIUM
Grind	9	
Mix	10	
Grate	11	

Powder	12	
Churn	13	
Blend	14	HIGH
Frappé	15	
Liquefy	16	

A Quick-Speed Guide for Everyday Uses (pages 14–23)

(Check speed comparison chart above for low, medium, and high ranges.) Note: This guide is for times when you are not following a specific recipe. With a few exceptions that call for the use of low or high speed, most foods are processed at medium speed. Although most of the recipe directions in this book coincide with this chart, there are a few instances in which the chart directions and the recipe directions vary due to the special nature of the recipe. *Always cover blender before blending.*

FOOD	DIRECTIONS AND STARTING AMOUNT	SPEED	TIME AND METHOD	YIELD
BEVERAGES				
Cocoa, hot (from mix or syrup)	Add liquids, then add mix or syrup. Follow package directions for amounts up to 1 quart.	low	about 5 seconds for 1 to 2 cups; 10 seconds for 3 to 4 cups	
Drink mixes (packaged) diet beverages, instant breakfasts, milk shakes	1 cup milk and 1 individual serving of mix.	low	10 seconds	
Dry milk (reconstituting)	Add water, then add mix. Follow package directions for amounts up to 1 quart.	low	10 seconds	
Frozen juice concentrate (reconstituting)	Add water, then add concentrate. Follow package directions for 6-ounce can.	low	5 seconds if thawed; longer if frozen	
Milk, flavored syrups, malted mixes	Add milk, then syrup or mix. Follow package directions for amounts up to 1 quart.	low	5 seconds for 1 to 2 cups; 10 seconds for 3 to 4 cups	
BREAD, CEREAL, COOKIES, CRACKERS, ETC. (crumbed for use in coatings, croquettes, meat loaves, casseroles, toppings, desserts, pies, etc.)				
Bread, dry	1 to 3 slices, broken into pieces	medium	on and off until crumbed or of desired texture	¼ to ¾ cup dry crumbs
Bread, soft	1 to 3 slices, torn into pieces	medium	on and off until crumbed or of desired texture	½ to 1½ cups soft crumbs
Cereal cornflakes, etc.	1 cup	medium	on and off until crumbed or of desired texture	⅓ cup crumbs
Cookies chocolate wafers	9, broken into pieces	medium	on and off until crumbed or of desired texture	½ cup crumbs

FOOD	DIRECTIONS AND STARTING AMOUNT	SPEED	TIME AND METHOD	YIELD
gingersnaps	8, broken into pieces	medium	on and off until crumbed or of desired texture	½ cup crumbs
vanilla wafers	12, broken into pieces	medium	on and off until crumbed or of desired texture	½ cup crumbs
zwieback	8, broken into pieces	medium	on and off until crumbed or of desired texture	½ cup crumbs
Crackers graham	7, broken into pieces	medium	on and off until crumbed or of desired texture	½ cup crumbs
soda (saltines)	14, broken into pieces	medium	on and off until crumbed or of desired texture	½ cup crumbs
round (2-inch diameter)	14, broken into pieces	medium	on and off until crumbed or of desired texture	½ cup crumbs
Potato chips	1 cup, coarsely broken	medium	on and off until crumbed or of desired texture	½ cup crumbs
Pretzels	¾ cup, broken into pieces	medium	on and off until crumbed or of desired texture	½ cup crumbs
BUTTER	2 cups heavy cream, sweet or sour	high	Pour into blender container; blend until butter forms. Salt if desired. Put into serving dish; refrigerate.	

FOOD	DIRECTIONS AND STARTING AMOUNT	SPEED	TIME AND METHOD	YIELD
CAKES				
White, yellow, chocolate spice (except angel food, chiffon, bundt, snack, or specialty types)	Follow package directions. Add liquids then ½ dry ingredients. Blend. Add remaining ingredients. Continue blending.	high	20 seconds, using rubber spatula to break surface of batter during mixing. Scrape down, then blend 10 seconds longer. Add remaining cake mix and continue blending for 30 seconds. Avoid overblending. Bake as directed on package.	
Gingerbread mix	Follow package directions. Add liquids then dry ingredients.	high	15 seconds. Scrape down. Repeat. Bake as directed.	
CHEESE				
*Hard (grated for use in toppings, casseroles, crumb seasonings, pastas, etc.)				
Parmesan, Romano	½ to 1 cup, cut into ½-inch cubes	medium	Start blender. Tip center cap and gradually add cheese.	½ to 1 cup grated
*Medium (grated for use in dips and spreads, casseroles, sauces, soufflés, breads, etc.)				
Cheddar, Swiss	½ to 1 cup, cut into ½-inch cubes	medium	Start blender. Tip center cap and gradually add cheese.	½ to 1 cup grated
Gruyère	3 to 6 wedges (1 ounce each) cut into pieces	medium	Start blender. Tip center cap and gradually add cheese.	½ to 1 cup grated
Soft (pureed for use in dips and spreads, cheesecake, other desserts)				
creamed cottage	1 to 2 cups. If cheese is dry, a small amount of milk or other liquid may be needed.	high	30 seconds. Scrape down and continue processing until smooth.	1 to 2 cups pureed

* For best results, make sure cheese is well chilled.

FOOD	DIRECTIONS AND STARTING AMOUNT	SPEED	TIME AND METHOD	YIELD
CHOCOLATE (grated for use in baking, sauces, etc.)				
Pieces	1 cup (6 ounces)	medium	Start blender. Add small amounts at a time.	1 cup grated
Squares	2 squares (1 ounce each), cut into quarters	medium	30 seconds	½ cup grated
COCONUT				
Fresh (shredded for use in curries, desserts, cakes, garnishes)				
	1 cup coconut meat, cut into ½-inch cubes	medium	Start blender. Add coconut, a few pieces at a time.	1 cup shredded
Coconut milk (for use in curries, desserts, drinks, etc.)				
from fresh coconut	1¼ cups hot milk 1 cup coconut meat, cut into ½-inch cubes	high	40 seconds	1⅓ cups
from canned or packaged coconut	1¼ cups hot milk 1 cup flaked or shredded coconut	high	40 seconds	1 cup
CREAM (for use in desserts, garnishes, etc.)				
*Whipped	1 cup heavy cream, chilled	low	Just until thickened.	1¼ cups thickened cream
* Blender will not whip cream to consistency of regular whipped. It will, however, thicken cream.				
DESSERTS				
Flavored gelatin	4-serving size package ½ cup boiling water 1½ cups cold water	low	Pour boiling water over gelatin in container. Cover and blend 5 seconds. Add cold water and blend 5 seconds longer. Pour into serving dishes or mold. Chill until set.	2 cups

FOOD	DIRECTIONS AND STARTING AMOUNT	SPEED	TIME AND METHOD	YIELD
Flavored gelatin, whipped (quick-chill method)	As above, substituting 1½ cups cracked or crushed ice for cold water.	low high	Pour boiling water over gelatin in container; cover and blend 5 seconds. Add ice and blend 30 seconds or until ice is liquefied. Pour into serving dishes or mold. Chill until set.	3 cups
Pudding, instant	Follow package directions. Add liquid then dry mix.	low	10 seconds. Pour into serving dishes.	
EGGS				
Hard-cooked (for use in salads, spreads)	3, whole and shelled	medium	Start blender. Tip center cap. Add eggs, one at a time. Blend until chopped or of desired texture.	1 cup chopped
Cooked yolks and whites (for use in spreads, garnishes)	4 yolks or whites	medium	Start blender. Tip center cap. Add yolks or whites, one at a time. Blend until chopped or of desired texture.	about ½ cup chopped
Raw (mixed for use in scrambling, omelets, etc.)	4 to 8 eggs	medium	5 seconds	
FROSTINGS (from packaged mixes— creamy type, not fluffy)	14-ounce package. Follow package directions, adding boiling water and butter to blender container first.	high	30 seconds, using rubber spatula to push ingredients toward blades	

FOOD	DIRECTIONS AND STARTING AMOUNT	SPEED	TIME AND METHOD	YIELD
FRUIT (chopped for use in spreads, cakes, desserts, etc.)				
Dried and Peels				
apricots, dried	½ cup	medium	Start blender. Tip center cap and add, one at a time.	½ cup chopped
figs, dried	4 medium	medium	Start blender. Tip center cap and add, one at a time.	½ cup chopped
peels (rind of lemon, lime, orange)	Cut thin rind off fruit. Cut rind in thin strips. Freeze solidly before chopping.	medium	Start blender. Tip center cap and add peel, one piece at a time.	
prunes, dried	½ cup, halved, pits removed	medium	Start blender. Tip center cap and add, one at a time.	½ cup chopped
raisins	½ cup. Freeze before chopping.	medium	Start blender. Tip center cap and add slowly.	½ cup chopped
Purees (for use in baking, desserts, special diets, baby foods, sauces, etc.)				
bananas	2 medium (ripe) sliced 1 inch thick. Add a little water, fruit juice, or milk if needed.	low	60 seconds. Push ingredients toward blades with rubber spatula. Repeat if necessary.	1 cup puree
peaches, canned	1 cup slices or 4 large halves with 2 tablespoons syrup	low	10 seconds or until smooth	1 cup puree
peaches, frozen	12-ounce package, partially thawed; drain off ½ cup syrup	low	10 seconds or until smooth	1 cup puree

FOOD	DIRECTIONS AND STARTING AMOUNT	SPEED	TIME AND METHOD	YIELD
pears, canned	1 cup chunks or 4 large halves with 1 tablespoon syrup	low	10 seconds or until smooth	1 cup puree
pineapple, canned	2 cups chunks with 2 tablespoons syrup	low	30 seconds or until smooth	1½ cups puree
plums, canned	1 cup, pitted, with 1 tablespoon syrup	low	20 seconds or until smooth	1 cup puree
prunes, stewed	1 cup (about 16), pitted, with 4 tablespoons syrup	low	20 seconds or until smooth	1 cup puree
raspberries, frozen	10-ounce package partially thawed; drain off ⅓ cup syrup	low	10 seconds or until smooth	¾ cup puree
strawberries, frozen	10-ounce package partially thawed; drain off ⅓ cup syrup	low	10 seconds or until smooth	¾ cup puree
ICE (cracked or crushed)	Fill container with 2 cups water; add ice cubes, one at a time.	high	about 3 to 5 seconds for each cube; wait until each cube is cracked or crushed before adding the next. When container is full, stop blender. Drain excess water.	

MEAT, POULTRY, FISH (ground for use in hash, croquettes, loaves, salads, spreads, etc.)

FOOD	DIRECTIONS AND STARTING AMOUNT	SPEED	TIME AND METHOD	YIELD
Beef, lamb, veal, pork, ham (cooked and chilled)	1 cup cubed; fat and gristle removed	medium	Start blender. Tip center cap and gradually add cubes.	1 cup ground
Chicken or turkey (cooked and chilled)	1 cup cubed; fat and skin removed	medium	Start blender. Tip center cap and gradually add cubes.	1 cup ground

FOOD	DIRECTIONS AND STARTING AMOUNT	SPEED	TIME AND METHOD	YIELD
Giblets (cooked and chilled)	1 cup, cut in 1-inch pieces	medium	Add pieces and cover with cooled cooking liquid; start blender.	2 cups chopped with liquid.
Fish, cooked	1 cup, broken up; skin and bones removed	medium	Start blender. Tip center cap and gradually add pieces.	1 cup ground
Fish, raw	1 cup, cut up; skin and bones removed	medium	Start blender. Tip center cap and gradually add pieces.	1 cup chopped

NUTS

FOOD	DIRECTIONS AND STARTING AMOUNT	SPEED	TIME AND METHOD	YIELD
Chopped	½ cup nutmeats	medium	3 seconds or until chopped to desired texture	½ cup chopped
Ground	½ cup nutmeats	medium	15 seconds or until ground	½ cup ground

PANCAKES AND POPOVERS (from packaged mixes)

FOOD	DIRECTIONS AND STARTING AMOUNT	SPEED	TIME AND METHOD	YIELD
Pancake mix	Follow package directions for up to 2 cups mix. Add liquids then dry ingredients.	medium	3 seconds or until mixed but slightly lumpy. Push ingredients toward blades with rubber spatula.	
Popover mix	Follow package directions. Add liquids then dry ingredients.	high	60 seconds	

SALAD DRESSING (from packaged mixes)

FOOD	DIRECTIONS AND STARTING AMOUNT	SPEED	TIME AND METHOD	YIELD
	Follow package directions, adding all ingredients at once.	low	15 seconds	1 cup

FOOD	DIRECTIONS AND STARTING AMOUNT	SPEED	TIME AND METHOD	YIELD
SEEDS				
Mustard, peppercorns, and other seeds	¼ cup	medium	60 seconds. Repeat if finer grind is desired.	¼ cup
Poppy	½ cup	medium	60 seconds or until crushed and moist	½ cup crushed
Sesame	½ cup	medium	60 seconds or until crushed and moist	½ cup crushed
SOUPS				
Canned condensed cream of tomato, mushroom, and other cream soups; split pea, etc.	1 soup can with 1 can water or milk. For sauces, use amount of liquid directed on package.	low	10 seconds	
SPICES (whole*) and HERBS				
Nutmeg	2 nutmegs	medium	60 seconds	2 tablespoons ground
parsley (basil, chives, dill, tarragon, etc.)	½ cup sprigs, coarse stems removed	medium	Start blender. Tip center cap and add a few sprigs at a time. Blend until chopped.	¼ cup chopped
* Not recommended: whole cloves, cardamon.				
SUGAR (pulverized for use in drinks)	1 cup granulated	high	60 seconds or until pulverized	1 cup pulverized
VEGETABLES (pureed for use in recipes, special diets, baby foods, etc.)				
Cooked or canned broccoli, carrots, peas, green beans, lima beans, etc.	2 cups, cut into pieces, with ¼ cup cooking liquid or 1 package (9 or 10 ounces) frozen vegetables, cooked. Add ½ cup liquid.	low	60 seconds or until smooth	1½ cups puree

FOOD	DIRECTIONS AND STARTING AMOUNT	SPEED	TIME AND METHOD	YIELD
Potatoes, instant mashed	Follow package directions for 2 to 6 servings. Place hot water, milk, butter, seasoning in blender container, then add potato mix.	low	Put all ingredients except potato mix into blender. Start blender. Tip center cap and add potato mix, blending until whipped.	

Raw (for salads, slaws, gelatin molds, soups, casseroles, vegetable dishes)

FOOD	DIRECTIONS AND STARTING AMOUNT	SPEED	TIME AND METHOD	YIELD
cabbage	1 medium, cut into quarters; remove core; cut into chunks. Fill blender container to 5-cup mark; cover with cold water.	medium	5 seconds. Drain. Repeat with remaining cabbage.	1 to 2 quarts chopped
carrots (for small amounts)	½ cup, sliced ¼ inch thick	medium	on and off until chopped	½ cup chopped
carrots (for large amounts)	2 cups, sliced ½ inch thick. Place in blender container; cover with cold water.	medium	5 seconds or until of desired texture. Drain.	2½ cups chopped
green pepper	1 medium, cut into 1-inch pieces	medium	on and off until chopped	⅓ cup chopped
mushrooms	1 cup whole, stem ends removed. If large, cut in halves.	medium	Start blender. Tip center cap and add, a few at a time. Blend until chopped.	1 cup chopped
onion	3 small or 2 medium, cut up	medium	Start blender. Tip center cap, add one at a time. Blend until chopped.	8 cups chopped
spinach	1 cup, torn in pieces, coarse stems removed	medium	Start blender. Tip center cap and add slowly. Blend until chopped.	½ cup chopped

Quickie Ingredient Equivalent Chart

4 ounces walnuts or pecans =	1 cup chopped nuts
2 slices soft bread =	1 cup soft bread crumbs
14 graham crackers =	1 cup graham cracker crumbs
28 saltine crackers =	1 cup cracker crumbs
24 vanilla wafers =	1 cup cookie crumbs
4 ounces Cheddar cheese =	1 cup grated cheese
Rind of 1 lemon =	1 teaspoon grated lemon rind
Rind of 1 orange =	2 teaspoons grated orange rind
1 medium apple =	½ cup chopped apple
2 medium stalks celery =	1 cup chopped celery
1 medium onion =	½ cup chopped onion
1 medium head cabbage =	8 cups chopped cabbage
2 medium carrots =	1 cup chopped carrots

The Devices on the Blender

There are several devices manufacturers have built into blenders that help to develop important blending techniques. These devices are designed for your cooking convenience. Many are found on the more expensive blenders. If you have them on your blender, understanding how they operate will help you to achieve the maximum results from your blender.

1 to 60-Second Timer

To operate blender with the timer, turn timer knob clockwise to desired time setting. Depress the correct speed button and switch on/off button to its on position. (To set timer for less than 10 seconds, turn timer knob beyond 10 and then set to desired time.) Your blender will do the rest, shutting itself off at the completion of the timed cycle.

Instant-Blending Capability—Insta-Blend®

Blenders with this device do exactly what the name implies. The motor turns on the instant you press the instant-blending —Insta-Blend®—switch and turns off the instant the switch is released. These switches are spring-loaded, which allows you to operate your blender for those very short periods of time required for coarse chopping (for example, nuts for brownies, cabbage for slaw), coarse crumbing, and other food preparation steps that require similar results. This feature gives you complete control to do these short-time blending operations by producing pulsating action of short starts and stops. The action moves food up and down, keeping it circulating and ensuring that the blades are fed properly. This feature is most convenient when working with small quantities.

If you have a timer model, you'll need to set the timer to the indicated number of seconds; otherwise, count the indicated number of pulses. If you don't have an instant-blending switch, operate the on/off control manually for the specified number of pulses.

Note: ▌ —Look for this symbol on certain recipes throughout the book. These recipes are adaptable to the instant-blending capability.

Food	Length of or Total Number of Pulses	Time in Seconds	Tips
(Manual-Touch Switch)			
Bread crumbs	5	15	one slice at a time—tear into pieces
Cabbage, dry	3	9	½ to ⅔ cup, cut up
Cabbage, wet	5	15	Fill container with cabbage; cover with water; cover, blend, and drain.
Carrots, chopped	3	9	1 medium, cut up
Cheese, grated	3	9	½ cup, cubed
Chocolate, grated	4	12	2 ounces, cut up
Cookie and cracker crumbs	4	12	6 to 8, broken up
Nuts, chopped	2	6	½ cup
Onion, chopped	1	3	½ cup, cut up

Blend-in, Store-in Containers—Blender Plus®

This feature in some manufacturers' models offers additional blend-in, serve-in, and store-in containers. Some models will also operate with Mason or canning jars or small jars designed for blender use, but exercise caution and make certain you follow specific instructions for the blender you are using to avoid breaking or shattering of jars.

Use these containers for reconstituting dry milk and frozen orange juice and mixing cocktails, milk shakes, salad dressings, marinades, and soups when you wish to prepare and store these items ahead of use. (You can also use them to aerate liquids like frozen orange juice to give a freshly squeezed flavor.)

12 oz   48 oz   16 oz

For best results, the blend-in container is not recommended for:

> *Solid foods, dips, spreads, and mixtures where additions are necessary during the blending operation or when a spatula is needed to redistribute ingredients.* The regular blender container should be used for these functions.
>
> *Hot foods.* The container may become too hot to grasp in your hand. With some plastic containers, hot liquid may spurt out when the lid is removed due to the pressure of the contents in the container.

To Freeze and Store

Some blend-in, store-in plastic containers can be stored, along with their contents, in the freezer. Always leave enough room in the container for expansion. Thaw by placing the container in the sink or on something to collect the condensation; then allow the contents to thaw naturally.

Note: ▌ —Look for this symbol on certain recipes throughout the book. It indicates recipes that are adaptable to the blend-in, store-in features.

Operating Your Blender for Best Results

As you experiment with your blender and the recipes in this book, you will discover many shortcuts and speed-ups for everyday cooking tasks.

You will probably notice that there may sometimes be a difference between the order of adding ingredients in blender recipes and your regular recipes. There is a reason for this. For example, in blender cookery, liquids usually go into the container before the solids; they help feed the solids into the blades and prevent "traffic jams." Solids that are to be *blended smooth* may be added piece by piece while the motor runs. Solids that are to be *chopped* and added to a mixture are added after the base is smoothly blended.

Because these and other differences are critical to achieving good results, follow these good blending tips:

- Always place blender on a clean, dry surface. Air circulation may carry foreign material or water into the motor.
- Make certain blender switch is in the off position when not in use.
- Secure blender container carefully onto motor base.
- It is a good idea to follow the specific directions for each recipe in placing ingredients into blender container. Be sure to cover blender container securely each time before turning it on.
- Always follow individual recipe and/or instructions for your own blender model.
- Always add liquid ingredients to the container before adding dry unless the recipe instructs otherwise, especially when crushing ice.
- When blending thick mixtures, blender container should not be more than half full. For thinner mixtures and liquids, it may be filled almost to capacity. When larger quantities are being processed, it is best to do part of the mixture at a time, empty into another container, then process more of the mixture.
- When chopping or pureeing solid foods, it is best to add a small amount at a time to blender container. Cut firm fruits and vegetables, cooked meat, fish, and seafood into pieces no larger than 1 inch. Cheeses such as Cheddar and Swiss are best cut in ½-inch cubes.
- Some vegetables, such as cabbage for slaw, are best chopped by the water method (covering the cut-up vegetables with cold water and then draining after processing). This is recommended for large amounts of chopped vegetables, as it saves time and ensures better texture.
- To liquefy fruits and vegetables, the water method is also used. Cut-up fruits or vegetables in the blender container are covered with liquid and then processed until all ingredients are liquefied.
- Add ingredients during the blending operation through the center opening of the cover by tipping the center cap.

If you have a one-piece cover and you want to add ingredients during the blending operation, cover the container with a square of heavy-duty aluminum foil that comes well down over the sides. Cut a hole in the center. If adding liquids, pour through a funnel fitted into the hole. To add solids, make an opening in the foil large enough to admit the pieces.

- When adding liquids such as oil in making mayonnaise, remove the center cap from the cover and insert a funnel in its place. This directs the flow of ingredients, thus preventing spattering.
- Control heavy mixtures with a small rubber spatula after removing the cover. Stop blender during processing and push ingredients towards blades with a rubber spatula if the blending stops.

A rubber spatula is helpful when:

1. Blending liquid and dry ingredients such as pancake batter, when some of the dry ingredients may cling to the sides of the container.
2. Blending thick mixtures such as dips and spreads. It helps the mixture go down into the blades.
3. Removing blended mixtures from container.

- Use the next higher setting if the motor seems to labor at selected setting.
- Always stop the motor before removing container from blender base, being sure to wait until the blade unit has stopped rotating.
- For real convenience, it is not necessary to wash blender container between steps in the same recipe unless the recipe so directs.

Controlling Texture

The various ranges between low, medium, and high *refine* the speeds and allow you to achieve the desired texture for a particular recipe.

The fineness or coarseness of ingredients in a finished mixture depends largely on the length of time the blender is run at a specific speed. The longer the blender runs, the finer the texture.

If you want a *creamy*, smooth base (sharp cheese blended with cream cheese, for example) with chopped pieces of another ingredient (such as olives or nuts), combine the smooth mixture first. Then add the other ingredient and run blender only until chopped to the coarseness desired.

For a *coarse* chop, turn blender to low for just a few seconds. Or run on low and turn off at once, repeating until texture is right (see instant-blending process, page 24).

Naturally, it is always wise to follow specific directions, as they have been tested for best results. However, generally speaking, it is best to use the lowest speed you can that will achieve the desired processed results. While speed settings for various blending jobs are recommended throughout the book, you'll begin to find the speed that suits you as you experiment with your blender and new recipes.

Controlling Time

The blender is incredibly fast, so be conservative about timing. Many jobs are done in 1, 2, or 3 seconds; slow operations generally require only 30 to 60 seconds. Remember, you can't unchop or unblend, so don't run the blender too long.

Remember that each recipe in this book recommends either *low*, *medium*, or *high* speed, whichever is required for each step in the process. If your blender has controls with different terminology, use the speed comparison chart (page 13) for checking the approximate range to follow.

Good Nutrition and How It Relates to Blender Cookery

Planning and Preparing Good Menus

There's more to a good meal than one exquisitely prepared dish. A memorable meal is balanced with contrasts of flavor, color, and texture. What's even more important, however, is the nutritional balance of a meal. We all know how important good nutrition is, but while we are more aware today than ever before of how nutrition affects health, we don't always practice what we know.

Physicians tell us that poor nutrition is due largely to poor eating habits. Proper eating habits begin at home with fresh, nutritious food that is properly stored and properly prepared. By getting into the habits of purchasing and preparing nutritious food and planning balanced menus—interesting in flavor, color, and texture—we can soon learn to *prefer* a nutritional diet.

The use of a blender and other electric appliances, such as a food processor, a mixer, and a slow cooker (to mention only a few), is an excellent way to assure nutritionally prepared foods and better snacks.

Blender cookery is healthful cookery. Foods high in nutritive value can be offered in a variety of interesting ways with blender recipes. With the use of a blender, there is little waste of nutritious ingredients. Vitamin-rich snacks, appetizers, salads, soups, sauces, and beverages can be processed in a matter of minutes—even seconds. Less handling and shorter cooking time of fresh ingredients mean less chance for a loss of precious nutrients.

Special Diets

When a member of the family goes on a special diet, blender preparation can create interesting food combinations and attractive dishes. A low-fat creamed soup, vegetable and egg, for example, may be blended together as a soufflé; as an omelet with a sauce; or as sliced, hard-cooked eggs in a vegetable sauce on thin toast. Plain cooked fruit may be used in a whip with custard sauce or as a puree to sauce an egg custard. Raw or cooked vegetables, cheese or fish, may be combined in a molded salad.

Snacking

It may be hard to control the urge to snack, but you can control what you find in the cookie jar and inside your refrigerator.

In the cookie jar, nutritious blender-made Apple Oatmeal Cookies or Cream Cheese Crisps are excellent choices for an evening snack or an after-school or work pick-me-up with a glass of milk.

In the refrigerator, keep crisp vegetables such as celery ribs, carrot sticks, green pepper slices, and cauliflower flowerets to accompany blender-made dips; keep all the ingredients for fruit drinks and milk shakes handy.

The Basic Four Food Groups

Most foods contain protein, carbohydrates, fats, vitamins, and minerals. However, some foods are richer in one nutrient than in the others. Planning a balanced menu requires paying attention to the different values of foods. There are four basic food groups, and a balanced menu will always include foods from each group. The following lists will help guide your thinking in planning nutritious menus.

1. Meat and Meat Substitutes

Each adult and child should have at least two or more servings per day of foods in this group. Meat, poultry, fish, shellfish, eggs, cheese, dry beans, and nuts all fall into this group. Their high protein content is essential for growth, energy, and replacement of body tissues; some of the B-complex vitamins, such as niacin and B_{12}, as well as minerals—iron, phosphorus, and sodium—are also found in these foods.

2. Milk and Milk Equivalents

Cottage cheese, pasteurized process or aged cheese, ice cream, sour and sweet cream, and yogurt are foods included in this group. Vitamins and minerals in this group, such as A, B-complex, D, E, calcium, and phosphorus are essential to building bones, teeth, healthy skin and eyes, and in the general normal functioning of the digestive tract. These foods also help resist bodily infection. Children under twelve need three to four eight-ounce glasses of milk a day; teenagers and pregnant women need four or more glasses of milk; nursing mothers need six glasses; other adults need two glasses.

Milk Equivalents

Cottage cheese	½ cup = ⅓ glass whole milk
Pasteurized process or aged cheese	1 slice or 1 ounce = ¾ glass whole milk
Ice cream	½ cup = ¼ glass whole milk

Keep in mind that nonfat, skim, or evaporated milk can be substituted for whole milk and that any milk used in cooking, on cereals, or added to beverages is considered as part of the daily quota.

3. Vegetables and Fruits

Everyone should have at least one serving every day of citrus fruit, tomatoes, or another good source of vitamin C and one serving of a green or yellow vegetable, which supplies iron, vitamin C, and other vitamins and minerals necessary for bodily growth and maintenance, absorption, and assimilation of other nutrients.

4. Breads, Cereals, and Other Grains

Everyone should have at least four servings every day of whole grain or enriched grain and cereal foods. These provide B-complex vitamins, vitamin E, fiber, iron, sodium, and other important nutrients necessary for assimilation of food for energy, nerves, skin, and the normal functioning of the digestive tract.

A Basic Formula for Planning Menus

1. Choose the main course first and plan the rest of the menu around it.
2. Select accompaniments such as an appetizer; potato, rice, or pasta; vegetables and/or salad; and garnishes, if desired.
3. Decide on bread or rolls.
4. Consider the ending for the meal—a beverage and dessert.

Remember that if your entree is a one-dish meal, you can team it with a special salad, some good bread, and a light dessert. One-dish meals are great and easy to plan.

Menu-Planning Hints

1. Plan menus around the basic four food groups. Keep all of the day's meals—including snacks—in mind for a total balance.
2. Select a light entree if your dessert is to be a rich, heavy one and, of course, select a light dessert if your entree is a heavy one.
4. Consider your food budget—plan menus around supermarket specials; splurge on one meal and budget the next; plan meals around leftovers.
5. Think about make-ahead meals—cook double batches, freeze extras, and make leftovers "planned-overs."
6. Experiment with new recipes and new ways to prepare foods.
7. Use your *blender* to short-cut many of the basic steps in the preparation of a dish or to make the entire recipe as far as possible.
8. Spark up inexpensive cuts of meat and other foods with blender sauces.

Menus

Look for the thoughtfully planned and nutritious menus in each chapter. They highlight the recipes in the chapters and combine with others throughout the book.

Appetizers

The term "appetizers" describes those foods designed to tempt the palate—canapés, dips, relishes, first-course salad mixtures, and hot hors d'oeuvres. Happily, these are the very foods that are often the most fun to prepare because they offer the greatest challenge to the imagination. The most exciting of them will be those you prepare yourself, with fresh, whole foods and seasonings.

For those of you who are short on time but long on creativity, your blender can become a third hand, helping you whip up delicious culinary masterpieces quickly and economically. With the help of your blender, you'll be able to create all the favorites—both new and old—contained in this chapter, ranging from Shrimp Pâté and Broiled Stuffed Mushrooms to a Parsley Cheese Ball and a Basic Sour Cream Dip. Many of these recipes are unusually versatile, such as the Roquefort Cheese Dip, which combines as well with crisp vegetables as it does with wedges of fresh pear and apple, or the Deviled Eggs, which, when served with thin slices of cucumber or zucchini squash, will provide a vitamin-packed midday or after-school snack.

Secrets to Making Appetizers

Plan suitable and sturdy accompaniments for dips. Ripply potato chips, corn chips, or a variety of small crackers and pretzels are excellent. For weight-watchers, always serve at least one vegetable dipper, such as thin slices of raw mushrooms or cucumbers; celery, carrot, or green pepper sticks; slices of zucchini; or cauliflowerets.

Elegant French-Style Picnic
Parsley Cheese Ball (page 39)
Chicken Liver Pâté (page 37)
Cold Asparagus Vinaigrette (page 121)
Crusty French Bread
Dry White Wine

Opposite: Broiled Stuffed Mushrooms, page 36.

BROILED STUFFED MUSHROOMS

1½ slices bread
½ cup cubed cooked ham
12 large mushrooms
1 small onion, cut up
3 tablespoons butter or
   margarine
2 tablespoons light cream
1 teaspoon prepared
   mustard
¼ teaspoon Worcestershire
   sauce
¼ teaspoon pepper

Heat broiler. Tear bread slices into blender container. Cover; blend at medium speed until crumbed; empty onto wax paper. Put ham into blender container. Cover; ◼ blend at medium speed until chopped; empty onto wax paper. Wipe mushrooms with damp cloth. Remove stems; set caps aside. Put mushroom stems and onion into blender container. Cover; ◼ blend at medium speed until chopped. Heat 1 tablespoon butter in skillet. Add mushroom-onion mixture; cook over medium heat, stirring occasionally, until onion is transparent. Stir in cream, mustard, Worcestershire, and pepper. Stir in bread crumbs and ham. Place mushroom caps on baking sheet, cavity sides down. Melt remaining 2 tablespoons butter; brush mushroom caps lightly. Broil 2 minutes. Invert mushroom caps; fill with ham stuffing; brush with remaining melted butter. Broil 3 minutes or until lightly browned. *Makes 12 stuffed mushrooms.*

36

OLIVE-FILLED CHEESE BALLS

½ pound sharp Cheddar
   cheese, cubed
2 tablespoons softened
   butter or margarine
½ cup all-purpose flour
Dash cayenne pepper
25 large, pitted ripe or
   stuffed green olives,
   drained

Heat oven to 400° F. Start blender at medium speed. While blender is running, tip center cap and gradually add cheese, blending until grated. Add butter, flour, and cayenne. Cover; blend at medium speed until smooth. If necessary, stop blender during processing and push ingredients toward blades with rubber spatula. Empty contents of blender onto wax paper. Shape about 1 tablespoon cheese mixture around each olive, covering it completely. Place on cookie sheet. Bake 15 minutes. Serve hot. *Makes 25 canapés.*

CHICKEN LIVER PATE

½ pound chicken livers
¼ cup butter or margarine
1 medium onion, sliced
2 hard-cooked eggs, shelled

¼ teaspoon salt
⅛ teaspoon pepper
⅛ teaspoon dried thyme

Cut livers in half; remove membranes. Heat butter in skillet. Add livers and onion; cook over medium heat, stirring occasionally, until livers are brown on all sides and onion is golden. Put one egg into blender container. Cover; blend at medium speed until chopped. Repeat process with second egg. Add half the chicken liver-onion mixture, salt, pepper, and thyme. Cover; blend at medium speed until chopped. Add remaining liver mixture. Cover; blend until mixture is smooth. If necessary, stop blender during processing and push ingredients toward blades with rubber spatula. Turn into serving dish. Chill. *Makes 1½ cups.*

37

SHRIMP PATE

2 cups cooked, shelled shrimp
3 tablespoons mayonnaise
2 tablespoons dry sherry
1 tablespoon lemon juice
½ teaspoon Dijon-style mustard

¼ teaspoon garlic salt
¼ teaspoon onion salt
¼ teaspoon ground nutmeg
Dash hot pepper sauce

Put shrimp into blender container. Cover; ◼ blend at
medium speed until chopped. Add remaining
ingredients to blender container in order listed.
Cover; blend at high speed until thoroughly mixed.
If necessary, stop blender during processing and
push ingredients toward blades with rubber spatula.
Turn into serving dish. Chill. *Makes about 2 cups.*

CHEDDAR AND PORT WINE SPREAD

½ pound Cheddar cheese,
 cubed
⅓ cup light cream
 3 tablespoons sweet port
 wine

¼ teaspoon onion salt
¼ teaspoon paprika
 Dash hot pepper sauce

Start blender at medium speed. While blender is
running, tip center cap and gradually add cheese,
blending until grated. Add remaining ingredients to
blender container in order listed. Cover; blend at
medium speed until smooth. If necessary, stop
blender and push ingredients toward blades with
rubber spatula. Turn into serving dish. Chill. *Makes
about 1 cup.*

ROQUEFORT CHEESE SPREAD

3 tablespoons milk
8 ounces Roquefort or blue
 cheese, crumbled and
 softened
1 thin slice onion
1 teaspoon Worcestershire
 sauce

¼ teaspoon hot pepper sauce
1 package (8 ounces) cream
 cheese, cubed and
 softened

Put all ingredients except cream cheese into blender

container. Cover; blend at medium speed until mixture is thoroughly combined. Add cream cheese. Cover; blend until smooth. If necessary, stop blender during processing and push ingredients toward blades with rubber spatula. Turn into serving dish. Chill. *Makes about 2 cups*.

Serving Suggestions: Serve with crackers or raw vegetables, or use to stuff celery.

PARSLEY CHEESE BALL

1 package (3 ounces) cream cheese, cubed and softened
6 pitted ripe olives
3 tablespoons dry sherry
½ teaspoon Worcestershire sauce

½ pound sharp Cheddar cheese, cubed
Dash onion salt
Dash garlic salt or powder
Dash celery salt
½ cup parsley sprigs

Put cream cheese and olives into blender container. Cover; blend at high speed until well mixed. Add sherry and Worcestershire. Cover; blend at high speed until smooth. Add Cheddar cheese and seasoned salts. Cover; blend at high speed until smooth. If necessary, stop blender during processing and push ingredients toward blades with rubber spatula. Turn mixture onto aluminum foil or wax paper. Refrigerate several hours or overnight. About 30 minutes before serving time, put parsley sprigs into blender container. Cover; blend at medium speed until finely chopped. Empty onto wax paper. Shape cheese mixture into ball; roll in parsley to coat completely. *Makes one 3-inch ball*.

Serving Suggestion: Serve with crackers or small rye bread slices.

DEVILED EGGS

8 hard-cooked eggs, shelled
1 tablespoon lemon juice
⅓ cup mayonnaise
¾ teaspoon onion salt
½ teaspoon dry mustard
½ teaspoon curry powder
  (optional)

½ teaspoon Worcestershire
  sauce
¼ teaspoon salt
⅛ teaspoon pepper

Cut eggs in half lengthwise. Remove yolks, being careful not to break whites. Put yolks and lemon juice into blender container. Cover; blend at medium speed until yolks are chopped. Add remaining ingredients to blender container in order listed. Cover; blend at medium speed until smooth. If necessary, stop blender during processing and push ingredients toward blades with rubber spatula. Fill egg white halves with yolk mixture. *Makes 16 deviled eggs.*

HUMMUS (Middle Eastern Chick-Pea Dip)

¼ cup tahini (sesame paste)
¼ cup lemon juice
3 tablespoons olive oil
1 or 2 cloves garlic, halved
1 can (20 ounces) chick-peas
  or garbanzo beans,
  drained

½ teaspoon salt
Dash pepper
Dash cayenne pepper
Chopped parsley

Put tahini, lemon juice, oil, and garlic into blender container. Cover; blend at high speed until smooth. While blender is running, tip center cap and gradually add chick-peas, blending until smooth. If necessary, stop blender during processing and push ingredients toward blades with rubber spatula. Add salt, pepper, and cayenne and blend until mixed.

Turn into serving dish; sprinkle with chopped parsley. Chill. *Makes 2 cups*.

Serving Suggestion: Drizzle top with olive oil and serve with sesame crackers or pita bread.

BASIC SOUR CREAM DIP

½ cup sour cream
2 packages (3 ounces each) cream cheese, cubed and softened

1 teaspoon Worcestershire sauce

Put all ingredients into blender container in order listed. Cover; blend at high speed until smooth. *Makes about 1½ cups*.

GUACAMOLE

2 ripe avocados, peeled and cut up
1 medium tomato, peeled and cut up
1 small onion, cut up

1 small chili pepper, cut up
2 tablespoons white vinegar or lemon juice
1 teaspoon salt

Put all ingredients into blender container in order listed. Cover; blend at medium speed until coarsely chopped. For smoother dip, continue blending until desired texture. *Makes about 2 cups*.

Serving Suggestion: Serve with cauliflowerets, celery sticks, cucumber slices, green onions, radishes, corn chips.

Many dips can be turned into spreads simply by reducing the amount of liquid and seasoning called for; conversely, a spread can be changed into a dip by increasing the liquid content and the seasonings.

Sandwich Spreads and Butters

Whatever you decide to spread on your sandwich, you can count on your blender to whip it up quickly and to a flavorful perfection. Besides helping you to make the recipes in this chapter, you can use the blender to create your own concoctions, blending bits and pieces of cheese, leftover meats, and odds and ends of relishes with mayonnaise, sour cream, cream cheese, or yogurt. You can use it to flavor butter with fresh herbs and condiments to spread on homemade breads or to top cooked vegetables. You can even use it to grind your own peanut butter for a spread that is super-nutritious. The base for these fillings can be as varied as the kinds of breads available. Try pita bread, toasted English muffins, fruit and nut breads; try sour black bread or rye or whole grain breads; try splitting a loaf of French bread down the center, spreading it, and then slicing it; try sourdough or Swedish limpa. To garnish a sandwich, think good nutrition and be imaginative. Substitute fresh spinach leaves for the usual lettuce and sliced avocado for the tomato; add alfalfa or bean sprouts; layer on sliced hard-cooked eggs and snipped chives.

Secrets to Making Spreads, Butters, and Sandwiches

A thin layer of butter spread on bread slices to be used for sandwiches will prevent sogginess. Soften the butter first so that it will spread more easily and go farther, and then spread the slices right to the edges.

Use an ice cream scoop to measure out salad spreads and other mixed fillings.

When toasting bread for sandwiches, avoid stacking the slices to prevent sogginess.

When blending spreads and fillings, stop blender when necessary during processing and push the ingredients toward the blades with a rubber spatula.

Opposite: Ham Salad Spread, page 44.

HAM SALAD SPREAD

1 cup cubed cooked ham
¼ cup mayonnaise
½ teaspoon prepared
    mustard

1 small sweet pickle, cut up

Put all ingredients into blender container in order listed. Cover; blend at medium speed until meat and pickle are chopped. If necessary, stop blender during processing and push ingredients toward blades with rubber spatula. *Makes about 1 cup.*
Note: Cooked corned beef or tongue may be used in place of ham.

CHICKEN SALAD SPREAD

¼ cup mayonnaise
1 small stalk celery, cut up
1 teaspoon Worcestershire
    sauce

¼ teaspoon salt
1 cup cubed cooked chicken

Put all ingredients except chicken into blender container in order listed. Cover; ◼blend at medium speed until celery is chopped. Add chicken. Cover; blend at medium speed until chicken is chopped. *Makes about 1 cup.*

Tropical Chicken Spread: Increase mayonnaise to ½ cup; add one can (8¼ ounces) crushed pineapple, well drained, and ¼ cup blanched almonds to blender container with chicken. Proceed as for Chicken Salad Spread. *Makes about 2 cups.*

TUNA SPREAD

1 medium dill pickle, cut up
1 hard-cooked egg, shelled
1 thin slice onion
1 can (6½ or 7 ounces)
    tuna, drained and flaked

⅓ cup mayonnaise
¼ teaspoon salt
    Dash hot pepper sauce

Start blender at medium speed. While blender is

running, tip center cap and gradually add pickle pieces, then egg, blending until both are chopped. Add remaining ingredients to blender container in order listed. Cover; blend at high speed until thoroughly mixed. *Makes 1⅓ cups*.

Salmon Spread: Substitute 1 can (7 ounces) red salmon, drained, boned, and flaked, for tuna. Proceed as for Tuna Spread.

BOLOGNA AND CHEESE SPREAD

½ cup cubed bologna
½ cup cubed American or
    Cheddar cheese
¼ cup mayonnaise

1 teaspoon prepared
    mustard
2 teaspoons pickle relish

Start blender at medium speed. While blender is running, tip center cap and gradually add bologna, blending until minced. Empty into mixing bowl. Repeat process with cheese, blending until grated. Add to bologna. Stir in remaining ingredients; mix thoroughly. *Makes about 1 cup*.

EGG SALAD SPREAD

3 hard-cooked eggs, shelled
¼ cup mayonnaise

¼ teaspoon onion salt
⅛ teaspoon pepper

Start blender at medium speed. While blender is running, tip center cap and gradually add eggs, blending until chopped. Add remaining ingredients to blender container in order listed. Cover; blend at low speed just until thoroughly mixed. *Makes about ¾ cup*.

Egg Salad and Bacon Spread: Cook three slices bacon until crisp; drain; crumble. Add to blender container with mayonnaise and seasonings. Proceed as for Egg Salad Spread.

NUTTED PINEAPPLE-CREAM CHEESE SPREAD

1 package (8 ounces) cream
    cheese, cubed and
    softened
2 slices canned pineapple,
    drained and cut up, or
    ⅓ cup canned crushed
    pineapple, drained

1 tablespoon liquid from
    pineapple
¼ cup walnuts

Put all ingredients into blender container in order listed. Cover; blend at medium speed until pineapple and nuts are chopped and mixture is thoroughly combined. If necessary, stop blender during processing and push ingredients toward blades with rubber spatula. *Makes 1¼ cups.*

46 RAISIN-CARROT SPREAD

¼ cup mayonnaise
½ cup creamed cottage
    cheese
Dash salt

Dash hot pepper sauce
½ cup seedless raisins
1 large carrot, pared and
    cut up

Put mayonnaise, cottage cheese, salt, and hot pepper sauce into blender container. Cover; blend at high speed until smooth. Add raisins and carrot. Cover; blend at medium speed just until raisins and carrots are chopped. *Makes about 1½ cups.*

PARSLEY BUTTER

¼ cup parsley sprigs
½ cup softened butter or
    margarine

1 tablespoon light cream or
    milk
¼ teaspoon salt

Start blender at medium speed. While blender is

running, tip center cap and gradually add parsley, blending until chopped. Add remaining ingredients to blender container in order listed. Cover; blend at low speed until thoroughly mixed. If necessary, stop blender during processing and push ingredients toward blades with rubber spatula. *Makes about ½ cup.*

Serving Suggestions: Use on broiled steak, cooked vegetables, corn on the cob, Italian bread.

Herb Butter: Substitute 2 tablespoons of a fresh cut-up herb, such as chives, tarragon, or dill, or a combination of fresh herbs, or 1 teaspoon dried herbs, for parsley. Proceed as for Parsley Butter.

Garlic Butter: Add one large clove garlic, halved, to blender container with parsley sprigs. Proceed as for Parsley Butter.

47

PEANUT BUTTER

1½ cups salted peanuts	1 to 2 tablespoons vegetable oil

Start blender at high speed. While blender is running, tip center cap and gradually add nuts, blending until finely chopped. Add 1 tablespoon oil. Cover; blend at high speed until smooth, adding more oil if needed. If necessary, stop blender during processing and push ingredients toward blades with rubber spatula. *Makes about 1 cup.*

Note: If using dry-roasted peanuts, increase oil as needed.

Nut Butter: Substitute salted cashews or mixed salted nuts for peanuts. Proceed as for Peanut Butter.

To make your own butter, see chart, page 15.

Beverages

A blender makes the best drinks ever—smooth and flavorful milk shakes, malteds, double frosteds—all the goodies you stood in line for at the soda fountain! With the addition of some ripe, succulent fruit or berries, either fresh or canned, flavor and nourishment will be enhanced even more.

Perhaps even more exciting is how fast you and your blender will be able to master all the frappés that boast crushed ice, not the least of which is the daiquiri—a chilly, frosted frozen daiquiri! Here is a time when a blender is a must.

The creation of an almost limitless number of beverage combinations is possible when you use a blender. In addition to the ever-present milk shakes and the frosted "spirited," or alcoholic, beverages are the super interesting and nourishing combinations of fruit and/or vegetable drinks—all rich sources of vitamins and minerals—such as Carrot Fruit Cocktail or Carrot Milk. Now, with the blender, you can bring the health bar right into your own home. Master these, add your own ingenuity, and you'll have opened up a whole new world of sipping pleasure.

Secrets to Making Beverages

Blending on the highest speed will make the smoothest beverage.

Melting chocolate is not necessary when making a drink that includes hot milk or hot water.

Add carbonated beverages just before pouring drinks from the blender container or after pouring into a glass.

In most instances, cracked or crushed ice should be used in blender beverages instead of ice cubes. If, however, there are more than 2 cups of liquid in your blender, you can add ice cubes one at a time while the blender is running, to cool, froth, or thin the beverage.

When preparing a blender recipe that calls for cracked or crushed ice, add it last and then process the mixture until it is smooth.

Opposite: Carrot Cocktail, page 50.

HOT COCOA

1 cup boiling water
¼ cup cocoa
¼ cup sugar

¼ teaspoon salt
½ teaspoon vanilla
3 cups hot milk

Put all ingredients except milk into blender
container. Cover; blend at low speed. While blender
is running, tip center cap and slowly add milk.
Serve immediately or keep hot in top of double
boiler. *Makes 4 to 5 servings.*

CAPPUCCINO

1 cup boiling water
1 cup hot milk
2 tablespoons instant
espresso coffee

Ground cinnamon or
nutmeg
Sugar (optional)

Put water, milk, and coffee into blender container.
Cover; blend at low speed until combined. Top each
serving with a sprinkling of cinnamon. Serve sugar
separately. *Makes 2 to 3 servings.*

CARROT COCKTAIL

2 cups pared, cut-up carrots
2 cups cold water
Parsley sprigs

Put carrots and water into blender container. Cover;
blend at high speed until smooth. Strain through
sieve, pressing with back of spoon to extract all
liquid. Serve over ice cubes. Garnish with parsley if
desired. *Makes about 3 cups.*

Carrot Fruit Cocktail: Substitute orange or pineapple juice for water. Proceed as for Carrot Cocktail.

Carrot Milk: Substitute cold milk for water. Proceed as for Carrot Cocktail.

FRESH TOMATO JUICE

¼ cup cold water
½ cup cracked or crushed ice
2 medium, unpeeled ripe tomatoes, cut up

½ teaspoon salt
½ teaspoon sugar

Put all ingredients into blender container in order listed. Cover; blend at high speed until liquefied. Strain through sieve, pressing with back of spoon to extract all liquid. *Makes about 1¾ cups.*

51

TOMATO-VEGETABLE COCKTAIL

1 can (18 ounces) chilled tomato juice
½ teaspoon salt
½ teaspoon Worcestershire sauce
Dash hot pepper sauce

1 thin slice onion
1 small stalk celery, cut up
¼ cup parsley sprigs
1 strip green pepper
1 cup cracked or crushed ice

Put all ingredients into blender in order listed. Cover; blend at high speed until liquefied. *Makes about 4 cups.*

Quick Family Breakfast on the Run
Wake-Up Breakfast Shake (page 54)
Raisin Toast
Coffee   Hot Cocoa (page 50)

FRESH APPLE JUICE

2 medium unpared apples,
cut up
1 cup cold water

½ cup cracked or crushed
ice
Sugar

Put apples, water, and ice into blender container.
Cover; blend at high speed until liquefied. Add
sugar to taste; blend until thoroughly mixed. If
desired, strain through sieve, pressing with back of
spoon to extract all liquid. *Makes about 1¾ cups.*

LEMONADE

2½ cups boiling water
½ cup sugar
½ cup lemon juice
2 slices lemon

2 cups cracked or crushed
ice
Mint sprigs or maraschino
cherries (optional)

Put water and sugar into blender container. Cover;
blend at low speed until sugar is dissolved. Cool.
Add lemon juice, lemon slices, and ice to syrup in
blender container. Cover; blend at medium speed
until well mixed and lemon is grated. Pour into four
tall glasses over ice cubes. Garnish with mint sprigs
or cherries if desired. *Makes 4 servings.*

FRESH PEACH NECTAR

½ cup cold water
½ cup cracked or crushed
ice
2 medium, ripe peaches,
peeled, pitted, and sliced

½ teaspoon lemon juice
Sugar (optional)

Put water, ice, peaches, and lemon juice into
blender container. Cover; blend at high speed until
liquefied. Add sugar to taste if desired; blend until
thoroughly mixed. Serve immediately. *Makes about
2 cups.*

Reconstituting Frozen Fruit Juice
Put one can (6 ounces) frozen fruit juice concentrate
into blender container; add required amount of water.
Cover; blend at low speed until completely mixed.

FRESH FRUIT FRAPPE

¼ cup chilled orange juice
½ cup cracked or crushed
ice
1 medium, ripe peach,
peeled, pitted, and sliced

½ medium, ripe banana, cut
up
Sugar (optional)

Put all ingredients into blender container in order
listed. Cover; blend at high speed until liquefied.
Add sugar to taste if desired; blend until mixed.
Serve immediately. *Makes about 1¼ cups*.

Note: Pineapple, strawberries, or other fruits may
be substituted for the peach and/or banana.

MILK 'N' FRUIT SHAKE

1 cup cold milk
1 cup fresh, frozen, or
drained canned fruit, cut
up
1 to 2 teaspoons sugar or 2
tablespoons honey
(optional)

1 teaspoon lemon juice
¼ teaspoon vanilla or ⅛
teaspoon almond extract
(optional)
1 cup cracked or crushed
ice

Put all ingredients into blender container in order
listed. Cover; blend at high speed until smooth.
Makes about 2½ cups.

Note: Fresh or frozen berries, fresh or canned
peaches or apricots, stewed pitted prunes, or
banana pieces may be used for the fruit. If canned
fruits are used, you may wish to omit sugar or
honey.

EGGNOG 🥤

2 cups cold milk	1 teaspoon vanilla
2 eggs	Ground nutmeg
4 teaspoons sugar	

Put all ingredients except nutmeg into blender container in order listed. Cover; blend at low speed until smooth. Pour into serving glasses; sprinkle with nutmeg. *Makes about 3 cups*.

Fruit Eggnog: Add 2 to 3 tablespoons frozen fruit juice concentrate to ingredients in blender container. Proceed as for Eggnog.

Creamy Eggnog: Add two scoops of vanilla ice cream to ingredients in blender container. Proceed as for Eggnog.

54 WAKE-UP BREAKFAST SHAKE 🥤

1 cup cold milk	1 egg
1 cup chilled orange juice	2 tablespoons honey or
¼ cup wheat germ or	maple syrup (optional)
cornflakes	

Put all ingredients into blender container in order listed. Cover; blend at medium speed until smooth. Serve immediately. *Makes about 2 cups*.

ORANGE FREEZE

1 cup chilled orange juice	1 pint orange sherbet

Put orange juice and sherbet into blender container. Cover; blend at high speed until smooth. *Makes 3 to 4 servings*.

Orange-Grapefruit Freeze: Substitute chilled grapefruit juice for orange juice. Proceed as for Orange Freeze.

Orange-Pineapple Freeze: Substitute chilled pineapple juice for orange juice. Proceed as for Orange Freeze.

Lemon Freeze: Substitute chilled lemonade and lemon sherbet for orange juice and orange sherbet. Proceed as for Orange Freeze.

CHOCOLATE ICE CREAM SODA

⅓ cup cold milk   Chilled carbonated water
½ cup chocolate syrup
3 scoops vanilla or chocolate
    ice cream

Put milk, syrup, and one scoop ice cream into blender container. Cover; blend at high speed until smooth. Put one scoop ice cream into each of two tall or soda glasses. Add chocolate mixture. Fill glasses with carbonated water; stir. Serve immediately. *Makes 2 servings.*

55

Strawberry Ice Cream Soda: Substitute one package (10 ounces) frozen strawberries, partially thawed, or 1 cup sliced fresh strawberries sweetened with 1 tablespoon sugar for chocolate syrup. Use vanilla or strawberry ice cream. Proceed as for Chocolate Ice Cream Soda.

Reconstituting Dry Milk Solids
Measure desired amount of water into blender container and add required amount of dry milk solids. Cover; blend at low speed until completely mixed.

VANILLA MILK SHAKE

1 cup cold milk   ½ pint vanilla ice cream

Put milk and ice cream into blender container. Cover; blend at high speed until smooth. *Makes 2 servings*.

Chocolate Milk Shake: Substitute chocolate ice cream for vanilla or add ¼ cup chocolate syrup to ingredients. Proceed as for Vanilla Milk Shake.

Strawberry Milk Shake: Add ½ cup sweetened, sliced strawberries to ingredients or substitute strawberry ice cream for vanilla. Proceed as for Vanilla Milk Shake.

Malted Milk Shake: Add 1 tablespoon malted milk powder to any of the above Milk Shakes before blending.

56

PEACHY SHAKE

1 package (10 ounces) frozen   2 tablespoons honey
    sliced peaches, thawed   1 pint vanilla ice cream
¼ cup lemon juice

Put all ingredients into blender container in order listed. Cover; blend at high speed until smooth and thick. Pour into three tall glasses. *Makes 3 servings*.

COCONUT-PINEAPPLE FLOAT

2 cups cold milk   ½ teaspoon vanilla
¼ cup moist shredded   ¼ teaspoon ground nutmeg
    coconut   ¼ cup crushed pineapple
1 tablespoon sugar   3 scoops vanilla ice cream

Put all ingredients except ice cream into blender container in order listed. Cover; blend at high speed until smooth. Pour into three tall glasses. Top each with a scoop of ice cream. *Makes 3 servings*.

THREE-FRUIT PUNCH

1 can (6 ounces) frozen
    lemonade concentrate
1 can (8¼ ounces) crushed
    pineapple

1 package (10 ounces) frozen
    strawberries, thawed
3 quarts chilled ginger ale
Ice

Put lemonade, pineapple, and strawberries into blender container. Cover; blend at high speed until smooth. Pour over ice in punch bowl. Add ginger ale. *Makes 4 quarts (32 four-ounce servings).*

GOLDEN MINT RECEPTION PUNCH

30 to 35 mint sprigs
2 cups sugar
2 quarts boiling water
2 quarts chilled orange juice
1 can (18 ounces) chilled
    pineapple juice

2 cups chilled lemon juice
1 bottle (28 ounces) chilled
    ginger ale
Mint sprigs and lemon
    slices (optional)

Put half the mint sprigs, 1 cup sugar, and 1 quart water into blender container. Cover; blend at medium speed until mint is chopped. Pour into a 1-gallon container. Repeat process with remaining mint, sugar, and water; add to container. Cool; pour through very fine strainer; chill. To serve, divide mint syrup and remaining liquids between two 1-gallon punch bowls; stir to mix and add block of ice to each bowl. Garnish with mint sprigs and lemon slices if desired. *Makes 7 quarts (56 four-ounce servings).*

1 ounce = 2 tablespoons
1 jigger = 1½ ounces or 3 tablespoons
Juice of 1 medium lemon = about 3 tablespoons
Juice of 1 medium lime = about 2 tablespoons

DAIQUIRI

3 tablespoons lime juice
3 ounces light rum
1 tablespoon sugar

½ cup cracked or crushed ice

Put all ingredients into blender container in order listed. Cover; blend at high speed until smooth. Pour into two cocktail glasses. *Makes 2 servings*.

Banana Daiquiri: Add ½ medium banana, cut up, to ingredients in blender container. Proceed as for Daiquiri.

Frozen Daiquiri: Increase cracked or crushed ice to 2 cups. Proceed as for Daiquiri. Spoon into sherbet glasses. Serve with straws.

RUM SWIZZLE

3 ounces dark rum
6 dashes aromatic bitters
3 tablespoons lime juice

2 teaspoons sugar
1 cup cracked or crushed ice

Put all ingredients into blender container in order listed. Cover; blend at high speed until smooth. Pour into two cocktail glasses. *Makes 2 servings*.

WHISKEY SOUR

3 tablespoons lemon juice
4 ounces whiskey
1 tablespoon sugar
½ cup cracked or crushed ice
1 orange slice, halved
2 maraschino cherries

Put lemon juice, whiskey, sugar, and ice into blender container. Cover; blend at high speed until well mixed and frothy. Pour into two whiskey-sour glasses. Garnish each with half an orange slice and a maraschino cherry. *Makes 2 servings.*

TOM COLLINS

3 tablespoons lemon juice
4 ounces gin
2 teaspoons sugar
1 cup cracked or crushed ice
Chilled carbonated water
2 maraschino cherries
2 orange slices
Ice cubes

Put lemon juice, gin, sugar, and ice into blender container. Cover; blend at high speed until smooth. Pour over ice cubes in two tall glasses. Fill glasses with carbonated water; stir. Garnish with maraschino cherries and orange slices. *Makes 2 servings.*

BLOODY MARY

6 ounces chilled tomato juice
3 ounces vodka
3 tablespoons lemon juice
¼ teaspoon salt
Dash pepper
Dash hot pepper sauce
¼ teaspoon Worcestershire sauce
½ cup cracked or crushed ice

Put all ingredients into blender container in order listed. Cover; blend at high speed until smooth. Pour into two cocktail glasses. *Makes 2 servings.*

ALEXANDER

2 ounces gin
2 ounces heavy cream
2 ounces crème de cacao

½ cup cracked or crushed
ice

Put all ingredients into blender container in order listed. Cover; blend at low speed until smooth. Strain into two cocktail glasses. Serve immediately. *Makes 2 servings.*

Brandy Alexander: Substitute 2 ounces brandy for gin. Proceed as for Alexander.

Coffee Alexander: Substitute 2 ounces coffee-flavored liqueur for gin. Proceed as for Alexander.

MARGARITA

60

1 strip lemon or lime rind
Salt
3 ounces tequila
1 ounce triple sec

1½ ounces lemon or lime
juice
1 cup cracked or crushed
ice

Moisten rims of two cocktail glasses with rind; dip rims in salt. Put remaining ingredients into blender container in order listed. Cover; blend at high speed until mixed. Pour into two cocktail glasses. *Makes 2 servings.*

GRASSHOPPER

2 ounces green crème de
menthe
2 ounces white crème de
menthe

2 ounces light cream
½ cup cracked or crushed
ice

Put all ingredients into blender container in order listed. Cover; blend at low speed until mixed. Strain into two cocktail glasses. *Makes 2 servings.*

STINGER

2 ounces white crème de
   menthe
3 ounces brandy

1 cup cracked or crushed
   ice

Put all ingredients into blender container in order
listed. Cover; blend at high speed until smooth.
Strain into two cocktail glasses. *Makes 2 servings*.
Scotch Stinger: Substitute 3 ounces Scotch
whiskey for brandy. Proceed as for Stinger.

HOLIDAY EGGNOG

3 ounces bourbon
1 ounce brandy
¼ cup sugar
3 eggs

2 cups cold milk
1 cup cracked or crushed
   ice
Ground nutmeg

Put all ingredients except nutmeg into blender
container in order listed. Cover; blend at low speed
until mixed. Strain into punch cups and garnish with
nutmeg. *Makes 8 to 10 servings*.

CREME DE MENTHE FRAPPE

2 ounces green crème de
   menthe

1½ cups cracked or crushed
   ice

Put crème de menthe and ice into blender
container. Cover; blend at high speed until smooth.
Pour into two cocktail glasses. *Makes 2 servings*.
Note: Any sweet liqueur may be substituted for the
crème de menthe.

Soups

A good homemade soup is always a welcome treat. With the blender to speed up preparation time and with inventive new ways to serve it, soup can provide an easy, quick, and satisfying meal. Offer a steaming bowl of Cream of Vegetable Soup on a brisk day; a cup of chilled Gazpacho on a hot one. Serve soup in mugs so it can be enjoyed in the living room, in the den, or on the porch; accompany it with a delicious appetizer or some tasty crackers. Use it as a perfect starter for a little dinner or, teamed with a crisp green salad and crusty bread, as a hearty main dish.

Soups also provide a natural setting for good nutrition. Those soups that contain milk and cream are good sources of calcium, protein, B vitamins, and vitamin D. Vegetable soups such as pea and bean supply protein, B vitamins, and iron. Of course, meat, poultry, and fish soups are also rich in protein and minerals.

Secrets to Making Blender Soups

For satin-smooth cream soups, blend liquids, vegetables, and any thickening ingredients at high speed until all solid particles disappear.

For soups in which ingredients are to be chopped, put soup liquid into blender container, add solids, and run on low speed for a few seconds.

For soups to be made in large quantities, divide liquid and solids into several portions, process each batch, then empty each containerful into the soup pot.

Summer Salad Luncheon
Chilled Cream of Watercress Soup (page 71)
Molded Chicken Salad in Lettuce Cups (page 157)
Cheese Popovers (page 135)
Lemon Chiffon Pie (page 216)
Coffee   Tea

Opposite: Gazpacho, page 70.

MUSHROOM SOUP SUPREME

¼ cup butter or margarine
½ pound mushrooms, sliced
2 cups chicken broth, or 2
    chicken bouillon cubes
    dissolved in 2 cups hot
    water

2 eggs
1 cup light cream
¼ teaspoon salt
⅛ teaspoon pepper
2 tablespoons dry sherry
    (optional)

Heat butter in skillet. Add mushrooms and cook over medium heat, stirring occasionally, for 5 minutes. Set aside six slices for garnish. Put chicken broth and remaining mushrooms into blender container. Cover; blend at medium speed just until mushrooms are chopped. Add eggs; cover; blend at medium speed for 2 seconds. Pour into saucepan. Add cream, salt, and pepper. Stir over low heat until hot and slightly thickened. Remove from heat and stir in sherry if desired. Garnish each serving with a mushroom slice. *Makes 6 servings.*

ONION SOUP

½ cup cubed Parmesan,
    Romano, or Gruyère
    cheese
4 large onions, cut up
⅓ cup butter or margarine
2 cans (10½ ounces each)
    condensed beef bouillon

2 soup cans water
¼ teaspoon pepper
8 slices French or Italian
    bread, toasted

Start blender at medium speed. Tip center cap and gradually add cheese, blending until grated. Empty onto wax paper; set aside. Put onions into blender container; add cold water to cover. Cover; blend at medium speed until onions are chopped. Drain thoroughly in colander. Heat butter in a deep, heatproof casserole. Add onions and cook over medium heat, stirring occasionally, until golden brown. Add bouillon, water, and pepper. Simmer, covered, for 30 minutes. Heat broiler. Top soup with toast slices; sprinkle with grated cheese. Broil, 4 to 5 inches from heat, for a few minutes or until cheese is golden and crusty. *Makes 8 servings.*

Note: For individual servings, cook onions in a medium-size, deep sauce pan. Add bouillon, water, and pepper; simmer, covered, for 30 minutes. Divide evenly into eight individual ovenproof bowls and proceed as for Onion Soup.

QUICK CLAM BISQUE

2 cups light cream or
    half-and-half
1 teaspoon celery salt
¼ teaspoon dried tarragon

Few drops hot pepper
    sauce
2 cans (7½ ounces each)
    minced clams with liquid

Put all ingredients into blender container in order listed. Cover; blend at medium speed until clams are finely chopped. Pour into saucepan; heat, stirring, until simmering. Serve warm or refrigerate and serve chilled. *Makes 4 servings.*

CRABMEAT BISQUE

2 tablespoons butter or
    margarine
½ small onion, sliced
1 package (6 ounces) frozen
    crabmeat, thawed, or 1
    can (6 ounces) crabmeat,
    boned and flaked
1 cup milk

1 tablespoon all-purpose
    flour
¼ teaspoon salt
    Dash pepper
1 cup light cream
3 tablespoons dry sherry
    Chopped parsley

Heat butter in medium-size saucepan. Add onion and cook over medium heat, stirring occasionally, until soft. Add crabmeat; cook over medium heat, stirring occasionally, for 1 minute. Put mixture into blender container. Add milk, flour, salt, and pepper. Cover; blend at medium speed until smooth. Return mixture to saucepan. Stir in cream; heat, stirring, until simmering. Remove from heat and stir in sherry. Garnish with chopped parsley. *Makes 4 to 6 servings.*

HEARTY BEEF SOUP

1 can (28 ounces) tomatoes
2 cans (10½ ounces each) condensed consommé
2 cups water
1 medium onion, cut up
4 carrots, pared and cut up
4 celery tops
4 sprigs parsley

6 to 8 peppercorns
3 tablespoons vegetable oil
1½ pounds ground beef
2 teaspoons salt
½ teaspoon sugar
⅛ teaspoon hot pepper sauce
1 bay leaf

Combine tomatoes, consommé, water, onion, carrots, celery tops, parsley, and peppercorns in large saucepan. Simmer, covered, for 25 minutes. Put half the mixture into blender container. Cover; blend at low speed for 1 minute or until vegetables are pureed. Pour into bowl. Repeat process with remaining mixture. Heat oil in skillet. Add ground beef; cook until browned, breaking meat up with fork as it cooks. Add soup; stir in remaining ingredients. Cover; simmer 20 minutes. Remove bay leaf before serving. *Makes 10 to 12 servings.*

DUTCH CARROT SOUP

4 medium carrots, pared and cut up
2 stalks celery, cut up
1 small onion, cut up
¼ cup butter or margarine
2 cans (14 ounces each) beef broth

3 tablespoons farina
1 teaspoon salt
⅛ teaspoon pepper
⅛ teaspoon ground nutmeg

Put carrots, celery, and onion into blender container. Cover with cold water. Cover; blend at medium speed just until chopped. Drain thoroughly in colander; reserve liquid. Heat butter in heavy saucepan. Add vegetables and cook over medium heat, stirring occasionally, until onion is golden. Add one can broth and one can reserved liquid; simmer about 8 minutes or until vegetables are tender. Put mixture into blender container. Cover; blend at low speed until pureed. Pour into saucepan. Add remaining can of broth, another can of reserved liquid, farina, salt, pepper, and nutmeg. Simmer, stirring occasionally, for 20 minutes. *Makes 6 servings.*

SPLIT PEA SOUP

2 cups split peas	1 clove garlic, halved
2 quarts water	1 bay leaf
Ham bone	2 teaspoons salt
2 medium onions, cut up	¼ teaspoon pepper
2 medium carrots, pared and cut up	¼ teaspoon dried thyme
2 stalks celery, cut up	Croutons (optional)

Rinse and sort peas. Place in large saucepan with remaining ingredients except croutons. Heat to boiling; reduce heat; simmer, covered, for 2½ hours. Remove ham bone and bay leaf. Remove any meat from ham bone; cube and reserve; discard bone. Pour half the soup into blender container. Cover; blend at low speed until pureed. Pour into bowl. Repeat process with remaining soup. Return all soup to saucepan. Add ham pieces; heat to simmering. Garnish with croutons if desired. *Makes 12 servings.*

PUMPKIN SOUP

2 cups chicken broth, or 2 chicken bouillon cubes dissolved in 2 cups hot water
½ green pepper, seeded and cut up
1 small onion, cut up
1 sprig parsley
¼ teaspoon dried thyme
1 can (16 ounces) pumpkin
1 tablespoon all-purpose flour
2 tablespoons butter or margarine
1 cup milk
1 teaspoon sugar
½ teaspoon ground nutmeg
½ teaspoon salt

Put 1 cup chicken broth, green pepper, onion, parsley, and thyme into blender container. Cover; blend at medium speed until vegetables are coarsely chopped. Pour into saucepan; simmer 5 minutes. Return mixture to blender container; add pumpkin and flour. Cover; blend at high speed until smooth. Pour into saucepan; stir in remaining 1 cup chicken broth and remaining ingredients. Heat to boiling, stirring often; simmer 3 minutes. *Makes 4 to 6 servings.*

CREAM OF TOMATO SOUP

1 can (28 ounces) tomatoes
4 sprigs parsley
1 small onion, cut up
1 stalk celery, cut up
3 tablespoons all-purpose flour
2 teaspoons brown sugar
1 teaspoon salt
½ teaspoon dried basil
⅛ teaspoon pepper
2 tablespoons butter or margarine
2 cups milk
Croutons or parsley sprigs (optional)

Put tomatoes with liquid, parsley, onion, celery, flour, brown sugar, salt, basil, and pepper into blender container. Cover; blend at high speed until smooth. Heat butter in saucepan. Stir in tomato mixture gradually. Cook over medium heat, stirring constantly, until mixture comes to a boil. Add milk slowly; heat gently just until simmering. Garnish with croutons or parsley if desired. *Makes 6 servings*.

CREAM OF VEGETABLE SOUP

2 cups milk
½ cup pared, cooked, cubed
    potatoes
1½ cups cooked or canned
    vegetables
1 thin slice onion
1 teaspoon celery salt

¼ teaspoon dried dill weed
    (optional)
⅛ teaspoon pepper
½ cup light cream
Salt to taste
Chopped parsley
    (optional)

Put all ingredients except salt and parsley into blender container in order listed. Cover; blend at low speed until smooth. Pour into saucepan; heat gently just until simmering. Add salt. Serve hot or chilled, garnished with chopped parsley if desired. *Makes 4 to 6 servings*.

CHEESE SOUP

3 cups milk
2 tablespoons butter or
    margarine
1 clove garlic, halved
½ pound Cheddar cheese,
    cubed
2 tablespoons all-purpose
    flour
½ teaspoon pepper

⅛ teaspoon ground nutmeg
1 cup chicken broth, or 1
    chicken bouillon cube
    dissolved in 1 cup hot
    water
½ cup light cream
Grated Parmesan cheese
    (optional)

Heat 2½ cups milk, butter, and garlic in heavy saucepan. Remove and discard garlic. Put remaining ½ cup milk, cheese, flour, pepper, and nutmeg into blender container. Cover; blend at high speed until smooth. While blender is running, tip center cap and gradually add hot milk mixture. Pour back into same saucepan. Add chicken broth and cream; heat over low heat, stirring constantly, just until simmering. Serve sprinkled with grated Parmesan cheese if desired. *Makes 6 servings*.

VICHYSSOISE

2 tablespoons butter or
  margarine
5 leeks, white parts only,
  sliced ¼-inch thick, or 1
  medium onion, sliced
2 cups pared, sliced potatoes
2 cups chicken broth, or 2
  chicken bouillon cubes
  dissolved in 2 cups hot
  water

¾ teaspoon salt
¼ teaspoon pepper
1 cup milk
¾ cup heavy cream
  Chopped chives

Heat butter in skillet. Add leeks; cook over medium heat, stirring occasionally, until tender but not brown. Add potatoes, broth, salt, and pepper. Bring to a boil; reduce heat; simmer until potatoes are very tender. Pour half the mixture into blender container. Cover; blend at high speed until smooth. Empty into bowl. Repeat process with remaining soup. Return all soup to saucepan. Add milk; heat just to boiling. Stir in cream. Chill. Garnish with chopped chives. *Makes 6 servings.*

GAZPACHO

1 can (18 ounces) tomato
  juice
1 clove garlic, halved
1 small onion, cut up
½ green pepper, seeded and
  cut up
1 small cucumber, pared
  and cut up
2 ripe tomatoes, peeled,
  cored, and cut up

3 tablespoons olive oil
3 tablespoons red wine
  vinegar
1½ teaspoons salt
¼ teaspoon pepper
  Croutons
  Chopped onion, green
  pepper, tomato, and
  cucumber (optional)

Put all ingredients except croutons and chopped-vegetable garnish into blender container in order listed. Cover; blend at medium speed until vegetables are finely chopped. Chill several hours or overnight. Top with croutons. Garnish with additional onion, green pepper, and cucumber if desired. *Makes 6 servings.*

BORSCHT

1 pint sour cream
1 thin slice lemon
¼ teaspoon salt
¼ teaspoon onion salt

1½ cups cooked or canned
   beets, sliced or diced
Sour cream (optional)

Put all ingredients into blender container in order listed. Cover; blend at high speed until mixture is smooth. Chill. Serve with additional sour cream if desired. *Makes 4 servings.*

CHILLED CREAM OF WATERCRESS SOUP

2 tablespoons butter or
   margarine
1 small onion, sliced
3 tablespoons all-purpose
   flour
½ teaspoon salt
¼ teaspoon pepper

2 cans (13¾ ounces each)
   chicken broth
4 cups watercress, coarse
   stems removed
1 cup heavy cream
Watercress sprigs

Heat butter in large saucepan. Add onion and cook over medium heat, stirring occasionally, until golden. Remove from heat. Blend in flour, salt, and pepper. Gradually stir in chicken broth. Cook, stirring constantly, until mixture thickens and comes to a boil. Add watercress and simmer 5 minutes. Pour half of watercress mixture into blender container. Cover; blend at high speed until smooth but still slightly flecked with green. Pour into large bowl. Repeat process with remaining watercress mixture. Add cream. Cover and chill thoroughly. To serve, garnish with additional watercress. *Makes 8 servings.*

Meat

The blender can become an important element in the preparation of meat dishes, especially in helping to develop distinguishing and characteristic flavors. Blend the gravy and vegetables in which Old-Fashioned Pot Roast has been simmering for 3 hours and you'll have a rich-flavored, smooth, and velvety sauce that you can achieve in no other way. Blend the chopped vegetables and seasoning for Sauerbraten before you add them to the meat and then add the gingersnaps after you've created the gravy—truly, a sauerbraten to bring raves! Chop cooked roast beef and special seasonings for a superb Roast Beef Hash. Or prepare a zesty marinade for Marinated Lamb Shish Kebabs, or a glaze for your next company roast.

Secrets to Meat Cookery

Know the meat cut you are cooking. The degree of tenderness will determine the method of cookery. Tender cuts (*rib, loin*) call for dry heat cookery. This includes roasting, broiling, pan-broiling, pan-frying, sautéeing. Less tender cuts (*chuck, brisket, flank, round*) call for moist heat cookery or cooking in liquid. This includes braising or cooking in small amounts of liquid, boiling, stewing.

Storing Meats: Before refrigerating prepackaged meats, unwrap them and rewrap them loosely in plastic wrap, wax paper, or aluminum foil, leaving the ends open to allow air to circulate.

If not frozen, ground meats and variety meats should be stored in the refrigerator immediately and then cooked as soon as possible—one or two days at the most after purchase.

Fresh meat, not prepackaged, should be removed from butcher's wrapping and wrapped as above.

Cured, smoked, and ready-to-serve meats also should be stored immediately in the refrigerator, although they may be left in their original wrappings.

All frozen meats should be defrosted in the refrigerator, in a microwave oven, or at room temperature before cooking. If you must use meat that is still frozen, allow additional cooking time.

73

Opposite: Blanquette de Veau, page 83.

OLD-FASHIONED POT ROAST

2 tablespoons fat or
   vegetable oil
5 to 6 pounds boneless
   chuck, rump or round,
   rolled and tied
2 teaspoons salt
¼ teaspoon pepper
1 can (10½ ounces)
   condensed beef broth
1 tomato, cored and
   quartered
1 medium onion, cut up

1 clove garlic, halved
2 carrots, pared and cut up
1 stalk celery with leaves,
   cut up
1 green pepper, seeded and
   cut up
1 bay leaf
2 tablespoons all-purpose
   flour (optional)
Salt and pepper
Chopped parsley
(optional)

74

Heat fat in heavy kettle or Dutch oven; add beef and brown on all sides. Drain off fat. Season meat with 2 teaspoons salt and ¼ teaspoon pepper. Add beef broth, vegetables, and bay leaf. Cover; cook over low heat about 3 hours or until meat is tender, basting meat occasionally with pan juices. Remove meat; set aside. Skim fat from gravy and discard; remove and discard bay leaf. Put gravy with vegetables into blender container. If a thicker gravy is desired, add the 2 tablespoons flour. Cover; blend at high speed until smooth. Season to taste. Leave meat whole or slice; return meat and gravy to Dutch oven to keep warm until serving time. Sprinkle with chopped parsley if desired. *Makes 10 to 12 servings.*

Dinner For A Crowd
Boeuf Bourguignonne (page 78)
Buttered Noodles
Green Salad Creamy French Dressing (page 165)
French Bread
Chocolate Mousse (page 188)
Coffee

SAUERBRATEN

2 tablespoons all-purpose
  flour
1 teaspoon salt
⅛ teaspoon pepper
4 to 5 pounds boneless
  chuck, rump or round,
  rolled and tied
2 tablespoons fat or
  vegetable oil
1½ cups water
½ cup vinegar

2 medium onions, cut up
2 carrots, pared and cut up
2 stalks celery, cut up
2 cloves garlic, halved
2 tablespoons brown sugar
1 bay leaf
¼ teaspoon ground
  cinnamon
¼ teaspoon ground cloves
½ cup seedless raisins
8 gingersnaps

Mix flour, salt, and pepper together. Rub meat well
with mixture. Heat fat in Dutch oven; add beef and
brown on all sides. Put water, vinegar, onions,
carrots, celery, garlic, and brown sugar into blender
container. Cover; blend at medium speed just until
vegetables are chopped. Pour over meat. Add bay
leaf, cinnamon, and cloves. Cover; cook over low
heat 2 hours. Add raisins. Continue cooking about 1
hour or until meat is tender. Remove bay leaf.
Break gingersnaps into blender container. Add 1 cup
gravy from pot roast. Cover; blend at high speed
until smooth. Pour into Dutch oven; heat to serving
temperature. *Makes 8 to 10 servings*.

SWISS STEAK

2 pounds boneless round
  or chuck, ½ inch thick
½ teaspoon salt
⅛ teaspoon pepper
2 tablespoons fat or
  vegetable oil
½ pound mushrooms, sliced
1 large onion, cut up

1 green·pepper, seeded and
  cut up
1 clove garlic, halved
1 can (8 ounces) tomato
  sauce
1 cup water
1 to 2 tablespoons
  all-purpose flour
  (optional)

Cut meat into serving-size pieces. Sprinkle with salt and pepper. Heat fat in heavy skillet; add beef and brown on all sides. Remove meat; set aside. Add mushrooms to fat remaining in skillet; cook, stirring occasionally, until lightly browned. Return meat to skillet. Put remaining ingredients except flour into blender container in order listed. Cover; blend at high speed until smooth. Pour over meat and mushrooms in skillet. Cover; simmer 1½ hours or until meat is tender. Remove meat to heated platter. Skim fat from gravy and discard. If a thicker gravy is desired, blend 1 to 2 tablespoons flour and a small amount of water to a smooth paste. Stir into gravy; cook, stirring constantly, until thickened. *Makes 4 to 6 servings.*

76 ## BEEF STROGANOFF

¼ cup butter or margarine
2 pounds beef tenderloin or
    sirloin, cut in thin strips
1 can (4 ounces)
    mushrooms, drained
1 large onion, sliced
2 tablespoons all-purpose
    flour
1 teaspoon salt

¼ teaspoon pepper
1 clove garlic, halved
1 can (10½ ounces)
    condensed beef broth
½ cup dry white wine
1 cup sour cream
1 tablespoon chopped
    parsley

Heat butter in large skillet; add beef and brown well on all sides; remove; set aside. Add mushrooms and onion to fat remaining in skillet and cook over medium heat, stirring occasionally, until onion is tender. Put mushroom-onion mixture, flour, salt, pepper, garlic, beef broth, and wine into blender container. Cover; blend at high speed until smooth.

Return meat to skillet; pour blended mixture over meat. Cover; simmer 15 minutes or until meat is tender, stirring occasionally. Stir in sour cream; heat just to boiling, stirring constantly. Sprinkle with chopped parsley. *Makes 6 to 8 servings.*

Note: Stroganoff is a good make-ahead dish. Simply prepare it up to the point before the sour cream is added. When you are ready to serve, reheat, stir in the sour cream, and bring just to boiling.

FONDUE BOURGUIGNONNE (Beef Fondue)

1 cup butter or margarine	1½ pounds boneless sirloin
2 cups peanut oil	steak, 1 inch thick, cut in
	bite-size cubes

Heat butter and oil together in saucepan over medium heat. When mixture bubbles, pour into 2-quart fondue dish or chafing dish. Set over heat source. Arrange beef cubes on serving platter. Provide fondue forks or disposable bamboo sticks for each person to spear cubes of meat. To cook, dip meat into hot oil mixture for a few minutes until meat is of desired doneness. Serve a choice of two or more of the following sauces for dipping:

Anchovy Sauce   (page 176)
Béarnaise Sauce   (page 175)
Mustard Sauce   (page 176)
Herb Butter, melted   (page 47)

Note: Cubed chicken, whole shrimp or scallops, or vegetables, such as mushrooms, carrot or zucchini chunks, green beans, and green pepper strips, may be used instead of or in addition to the beef.

BOEUF BOURGUIGNONNE
(Braised Beef in Burgundy)

4 pounds boneless chuck or
    round, cut in 1½-inch
    cubes
½ cup all-purpose flour
1 teaspoon salt
½ teaspoon pepper
½ cup fat or vegetable oil
3 cups Burgundy
1 bay leaf
1 can (10½ ounces)
    condensed beef broth

2 teaspoons tomato paste
¼ cup parsley sprigs
1 large onion, cut up
2 carrots, pared and cut up
2 cloves garlic, halved
½ teaspoon dried thyme
12 to 16 small white onions,
    peeled

Dredge beef in mixture of flour, salt, and pepper.
Reserve remaining flour mixture. Heat fat in heavy
skillet or Dutch oven. Add meat; brown well on all
sides. Add wine and bay leaf. Heat oven to 325° F.
Put beef broth, tomato paste, parsley, onion,
carrots, garlic, and thyme into blender container.
Cover; blend at medium speed just until vegetables
are chopped. Pour over meat; cover. Cook in oven
1½ hours. Add small white onions. Continue
cooking 1½ hours or until beef is tender. *Makes 8
servings.*

78

ROAST BEEF HASH

3 cups cubed cooked roast
    beef
1 medium onion, cut up
½ cup light cream
1 teaspoon salt

¼ teaspoon pepper
2 cups pared, sliced boiled
    potatoes
2 tablespoons butter or
    margarine

Start blender at high speed. While blender is

running, tip center cap and gradually add 1 cup meat cubes, blending until ground. Empty into bowl. Repeat process until all beef has been ground. Put onion, cream, salt, and pepper into blender container. Cover; blend at medium speed until onion is chopped. While blender is running, tip center cap and gradually add potatoes, blending until ground. If necessary, stop blender during processing and push ingredients toward blades with rubber spatula. Add to meat in bowl; mix thoroughly. Heat butter in large skillet. Add meat mixture; spread evenly over bottom of pan. Cook over low heat about 15 minutes or until browned on bottom. Turn; brown second side about 10 minutes. If a browner crust is desired, turn again and continue cooking. *Makes 4 to 6 servings.*

79

How to Chop Raw Meat in the Blender

Tear one-quarter of a slice of white bread into blender container. Add ½ cup cubed raw meat with all gristle and heavy connective tissue removed. (You may add a small piece of onion at this point if you wish.) Cover; blend at medium speed until meat is chopped. If necessary, start and stop blender to toss meat toward blades or use an instant-blending process if your blender has this convenience (see page 24). Empty onto wax paper; shape into a meat patty or use in a recipe.

OLD-FASHIONED MEAT LOAF

1 pound ground chuck or
   round
½ pound ground pork
½ pound ground veal
5 slices bread
¼ cup milk
1 small onion, cut up
½ green pepper, seeded and
   cut up

¼ cup catsup
1 teaspoon Worcestershire
   sauce
1 egg
2 teaspoons salt
¼ teaspoon pepper

Heat oven to 350° F. Combine chuck, pork, and veal in large bowl. Tear two slices bread into blender container. Cover; blend at medium speed until crumbed. Add to meat. Repeat process until all bread is crumbed. Put remaining ingredients into blender container in order listed. Cover; blend at medium speed until vegetables are chopped. Pour over meat; mix gently but thoroughly. Pack meat mixture into greased 9 x 5 x 3-inch loaf pan. Bake 1¼ hours. Serve hot or cold. *Makes 6 servings.*

SWEDISH MEATBALLS

¾ pound ground chuck or
   round
¼ pound ground pork
¼ pound ground veal
3 slices bread
1 cup milk
1 small onion, cut up
1 egg
1½ teaspoons salt
¼ teaspoon pepper

¼ teaspoon ground nutmeg
3 tablespoons butter or
   margarine
3 tablespoons all-purpose
   flour
1 teaspoon sugar
1 cup water
1 cup light cream
1 beef bouillon cube

Combine beef, pork, and veal in large bowl. Tear

bread slices into blender container. Add milk, onion, egg, ½ teaspoon salt, ⅛ teaspoon pepper, and nutmeg. Cover; blend at high speed until smooth. Add to meat mixture; mix thoroughly. Shape into 1-inch balls. Heat 2 tablespoons butter in large skillet; add half the meatballs. Brown well on all sides; remove. Repeat with remaining 1 tablespoon butter and remaining meatballs. Remove. Scrape brown bits from bottom of skillet; put bits and pan juices into blender container. Add flour, sugar, water, cream, bouillon cube, remaining 1 teaspoon salt, and ⅛ teaspoon pepper. Cover; blend at high speed until smooth. Pour into skillet; cook, stirring constantly, until thickened. Add meatballs; simmer over low heat about 5 minutes. *Makes 4 to 6 servings.*

81

Casual Get Together
Basic Sour Cream Dip (page 41)   Crisp Raw Vegetables
Chili Con Carne (page 81)   Fluffy Rice
Green Salad   French Dressing (page 165)
Golden Corn Muffins (page 138)
Baked Custard (page 190)
Coffee

CHILI CON CARNE

2 tablespoons fat or vegetable oil

1½ pounds ground chuck or round

3 medium onions, cut up

1 large green pepper, seeded and cut up

1 can (28 ounces) tomatoes

1½ teaspoons salt

1 to 2 tablespoons chili powder

1 teaspoon powdered cumin

½ teaspoon paprika

¼ teaspoon ground cloves

¼ teaspoon hot pepper sauce

1 can (about 16 ounces) red kidney beans

Heat fat in heavy skillet. Add meat; cook, breaking up with spoon or fork, until brown. Put remaining ingredients except kidney beans into blender container in order listed. Cover; blend at medium speed until smooth. Add to meat in skillet. Cover; simmer 2 hours, adding a little hot water if mixture becomes too thick. Add beans; heat thoroughly. *Makes 4 to 6 servings.*

VEAL BIRDS

6 slices veal for scallopine (1½ pounds)
4 slices bread
1 medium onion, cut up
½ teaspoon salt
¼ teaspoon pepper
4 sprigs parsley
¼ cup melted butter or margarine

1 can (10½ ounces) condensed beef broth
All-purpose flour
¼ cup butter or margarine
½ teaspoon dried thyme
½ teaspoon dried oregano
1 tablespoon all-purpose flour
½ cup water

Pound veal slices to ¼-inch thickness. Set aside. Tear two slices bread into blender container; add onion. Cover; blend at medium speed until onion is chopped. Empty into bowl. Tear remaining two slices bread into blender container; add salt, pepper, and parsley. Cover; blend at medium speed until bread is crumbed. Add to onion mixture. Stir in melted butter and ¼ cup beef broth. Divide mixture evenly among veal slices; roll up; tie with clean string in several places to hold together. Roll in flour; shake off excess. Heat ¼ cup butter in skillet; brown birds well on all sides; remove; keep warm. Stir thyme, oregano, and 1 tablespoon flour into fat in skillet. Add water and remaining beef broth. Stir to loosen brown bits on sides of pan; stir rapidly over medium heat until thickened and bubbly. Return birds to skillet. Cover; simmer over low heat 10 minutes. Snip string carefully from each bird. *Makes 6 servings.*

BLANQUETTE DE VEAU
(Veal Stew)

1 cup water
1 medium onion, cut up
1 carrot, pared and cut up
3 sprigs parsley
½ cup all-purpose flour
1 teaspoon salt
¼ teaspoon ground cloves
¼ teaspoon dried thyme
¼ teaspoon pepper
1 bay leaf

2 pounds veal shoulder, cut in 1-inch cubes
12 small white onions, peeled
½ pound button mushrooms
½ cup heavy cream
2 egg yolks
2 teaspoons lemon juice
Chopped parsley (optional)

Put water, onion, carrot, parsley, flour, salt, cloves, thyme, pepper, and bay leaf into blender container. Cover; blend at medium speed until vegetables are chopped. Put veal and small white onions into large kettle or Dutch oven; add blended mixture. Cover; simmer 1 hour, stirring occasionally. Wipe mushrooms with damp cloth and add to stew; cover; simmer 30 minutes, stirring occasionally. Put cream, egg yolks, and lemon juice into blender container. Add about ½ cup hot liquid from veal. Cover; blend at high speed until smooth. Stir into liquid in kettle. Cook over low heat, stirring constantly, about 3 minutes or just until sauce bubbles. Do not allow sauce to boil. Sprinkle with chopped parsley if desired. *Makes 6 servings.*

VITELLO TONNATO
(Cold Veal with Tuna Sauce)

2 or 3 tablespoons olive oil
3 pounds boneless rolled leg
   or rump of veal
2 medium carrots, pared
   and cut up
2 stalks celery, cut up
1 medium onion, cut up
3 sprigs parsley
1 clove garlic, halved
2 bay leaves
2 whole peppercorns

Pinch dried thyme
1 can (2 ounces) flat
   anchovy fillets, drained
1 can (6½ or 7 ounces)
   tuna, drained and flaked
1¼ cups dry white wine
2 tablespoons capers,
   drained
1 cup mayonnaise
Capers and chopped
   parsley (optional)

84

Heat 2 tablespoons oil in Dutch oven. Add veal;
brown lightly on all sides. Put carrots, celery, onion,
parsley, and garlic into blender container. Add cold
water to cover vegetables. Cover; blend at medium
speed just until vegetables are chopped. Drain
thoroughly in colander. Add to veal; cook about 10
minutes, stirring occasionally, until vegetables are
tender. Add an additional tablespoon olive oil if
necessary. Add bay leaves, peppercorns, thyme,
anchovies, tuna, and wine. Cover; simmer 1¾ to 2
hours or until veal is tender. Remove meat from
Dutch oven; cool; wrap in aluminum foil;
refrigerate. Measure sauce; if necessary, return
sauce to pan and boil rapidly until reduced to 3
cups. Discard bay leaves and peppercorns. Chill
sauce. When ready to serve, pour sauce into
blender container; add 2 tablespoons capers and
mayonnaise. Cover; blend at high speed until
smooth. Slice veal; serve with sauce. Garnish with
additional capers and chopped parsley if desired.
Makes 8 servings.

PORK CHOPS WITH ORANGE DRESSING

4 pork chops, each 1 inch
   thick
2 tablespoons all-purpose
   flour
2 teaspoons salt
½ teaspoon paprika
¼ teaspoon pepper
1 tablespoon fat or
   vegetable oil

6 slices bread, crusts
   removed
Rind from one medium
   orange, cut up
1 stalk celery, cut up
1 small onion, cut up
1 teaspoon sugar
¼ teaspoon dried thyme
½ cup orange juice

Heat oven to 350° F. Dredge pork chops with
mixture of flour, 1 teaspoon salt, paprika, and ⅛
teaspoon pepper. Heat fat in large, heavy skillet;
add chops and brown on both sides. Tear one slice
bread into blender container; add orange rind.
Cover; ⊓ blend at medium speed until bread is
crumbed and orange rind is grated. Empty into
bowl. Repeat process with remaining bread, one
slice at a time; empty crumbs into bowl. Put celery
and onion into blender container. Cover; blend at
medium speed until chopped. Add to bread crumbs;
add remaining 1 teaspoon salt, ⅛ teaspoon pepper,
sugar, and thyme; mix lightly. Arrange chops in
single layer in shallow baking dish. Heap one-fourth
of the dressing on each chop. Pour orange juice into
skillet; stir to dissolve any brown particles; pour
liquid around chops. Cover baking dish. Bake 45
minutes. Uncover; bake 15 minutes or until chops
are tender. *Makes 4 servings.*

85

LUAU RIBS

4 pounds spareribs, cut in
  serving-size pieces
1 can (1 pound) sliced
  peaches, drained
½ cup firmly packed brown
  sugar
⅓ cup catsup

⅓ cup vinegar
2 tablespoons soy sauce
2 cloves garlic, halved
2 teaspoons ground ginger
1 teaspoon salt
Dash pepper

Heat oven to 450° F. Place spareribs, meaty side up,
in shallow baking pan. Bake 45 minutes; pour off fat
and discard. Put remaining ingredients into blender
container in order listed. Cover; blend at high speed
until smooth. Pour over ribs. Reduce oven
temperature to 350° F. Bake 1 hour or until done,
basting ribs with sauce several times. *Makes 4
servings.*

CARAMEL-GLAZED ORANGE HAM LOAF

4 cups cubed cooked ham
5 slices bread
3 eggs
½ small onion, cut up
½ cup frozen orange juice
  concentrate, thawed
⅓ cup water

1 teaspoon dry mustard
⅛ teaspoon pepper
⅓ cup firmly packed brown
  sugar
1 teaspoon whole cloves
Orange slices and chopped
  parsley (optional)

Heat oven to 350° F. Start blender at high speed.
While blender is running, tip center cap and
gradually add 1 cup ham cubes, blending until
ground. Empty into bowl. Repeat process with
remaining ham. Tear two slices bread into blender
container. Cover; blend at medium speed until
crumbed. Empty onto wax paper. Repeat with
remaining bread until all is crumbed. Put eggs,
onion, orange juice concentrate, water, mustard,
and pepper into blender container. Cover; blend at

low speed until mixed. Add to ground ham; mix thoroughly. Sprinkle brown sugar and cloves over bottom of 9 x 5 x 3-inch loaf pan. Spoon ham mixture into pan. Bake 50 to 55 minutes. Turn out onto serving platter. Garnish with orange slices and parsley if desired. *Makes 6 to 8 servings.*

SWEET AND SOUR PORK

10 gingersnaps	1 tablespoon sugar
2 medium onions, cut up	1½ teaspoons salt
2 tablespoons fat or vegetable oil	½ cup drained pineapple chunks
⅓ cup vinegar	⅓ cup seedless raisins
2 cups water	2 cups cubed cooked pork

Break three or four gingersnaps into blender container. Cover; blend at medium speed until crumbed. Empty onto wax paper. Repeat process until all gingersnaps have been crumbed; set aside. Put one onion into blender container. Cover; blend at medium speed until chopped. Empty into small bowl. Repeat process with second onion. Heat fat in large, heavy skillet; add onions and cook over medium heat, stirring occasionally, until lightly browned. Add gingersnap crumbs, vinegar, water, sugar, and salt. Cook, stirring occasionally, until thick and smooth. Add remaining ingredients; simmer 15 minutes. *Makes 4 servings.*

How to Tenderize Less Tender Cuts of Meat
Prepare a marinade using oil and lemon juice, vinegar, or wine; season with herbs, spices, onion, or garlic. Let less tender cuts of meat marinate for several hours or overnight.

STUFFED CROWN ROAST OF LAMB

12 to 16-rib crown lamb roast
   (6 to 8 pounds)
   Salt and pepper

Apple-Prune Stuffing
   (page 99)

Heat oven to 325° F. Wrap rib ends of roast with aluminum foil to prevent charring. Season meat with salt and pepper. Place roast, bone ends up, on rack in roasting pan. Spoon Apple-Prune Stuffing into center. Insert meat thermometer between ribs into center of thickest part of meat. Roast until thermometer registers 175° F. for medium done or 180° F. for well done (it will take about 35 to 40 minutes per pound). If you prefer lamb slightly pink, roast only until thermometer registers 170° F. Baste top of stuffing occasionally with pan juices. When roast is done, place on heated platter. Remove aluminum foil from ribs; top each rib with paper frill if desired. *Makes 6 to 8 servings.*

Note: Cover stuffing with aluminum foil if it begins to overbrown.

SAVORY LEG OF LAMB

1 leg of lamb (5 to 6
   pounds)
1 cup dry white wine
1 medium onion, cut up
⅔ cup olive oil
1 clove garlic, halved

Thin strip lemon rind
½ teaspoon dried rosemary
½ teaspoon dried thyme
½ teaspoon salt
¼ teaspoon pepper

Place meat in deep glass or enamel baking dish. Put remaining ingredients into blender container in order listed. Cover; blend at medium speed until onion is finely chopped. Pour over meat. Cover; refrigerate at least 24 hours, turning meat occasionally. Heat oven to 450° F. Lift meat from marinade; let drain. Place lamb, fat side up, on rack in shallow roasting pan. Insert meat thermometer into thickest part of meat. Roast 15 minutes. Reduce oven temperature to 350° F. Pour marinade over meat. Roast until meat thermometer registers 170° F. for slightly rare, 175° F. for medium done, or 180° F. for well done. Baste roast frequently with marinade while cooking. Add a few tablespoons boiling water to pan during roasting if juices cook down too quickly. *Makes 8 to 10 servings.*

MARINATED LAMB SHISH KEBABS

1 cup dry white wine
¼ cup tarragon vinegar
⅔ cup olive or vegetable oil
1 teaspoon salt
1 medium onion, cut up
1 teaspoon dried marjoram
1 teaspoon dried rosemary
1½ pounds lamb shoulder or
    leg, cut in 1½-inch cubes

8 small white onions, peeled
    and parboiled
1 green pepper, seeded and
    cut in 8 pieces
2 tomatoes, cored and
    quartered

Put wine, vinegar, oil, salt, onion, marjoram, and rosemary into blender container. Cover; blend at medium speed until onion is chopped. Place meat in glass or enamel baking dish; pour marinade over lamb. Cover; refrigerate several hours or overnight. Heat broiler. On each of four skewers, thread meat cubes and vegetables, dividing evenly. Brush vegetables with marinade. Broil kebabs 12 to 15 minutes, turning to brown all sides. Baste with remaining marinade during broiling. *Makes 4 servings.*

Beef Shish Kebabs: Substitute 1½ pounds beef sirloin or round for lamb. Proceed as for Marinated Lamb Shish Kebabs.

Poultry

Part of the secret of poultry's popularity is its versatility. It can be cooked in almost any way you can think of—fried, stewed, braised, broiled, poached, baked, or grilled. Regardless of how you choose to cook your poultry, though, its flavor will be greatly enhanced through the use of your blender.

Try Twin Braised Chickens with Cashew-Rice Stuffing—a dish that boasts a flavorful rice stuffing cooked in white wine and chicken broth combined with a mixture of blender-chopped cashews, vegetables, and herbs. Consider Chicken Normandy. Redolent with chopped apples, onions, and celery, it is browned, brandied, and flamed, then seasoned and cooked. Everybody's favorite, Chicken Croquettes, also relies heavily on the blender.

Secrets to Poultry Cookery

Select plump chickens with creamy, moist, pale pink, skin and fresh, clear, yellow fat.

Remove uncooked fresh chicken from original wrappings and wrap loosely in wax paper or plastic wrap. Store in coldest part of refrigerator and use within three days.

Store purchased, already frozen chicken in freezer until ready for use.

Wrap fresh poultry to be frozen in proper freezer wraps.

Allow the following amounts per serving:

Chicken
For frying, roasting, or stewing—¾ to 1 pound
For broiling—one-quarter to one-half chicken
Rock Cornish Hens—one bird
Duckling—one-quarter duckling
Turkey—about ¾ pound

Follow directions for timing poultry. Overcooking can impair flavor and texture.

Store leftover poultry in refrigerator immediately. Any stuffing should be removed from bird and refrigerated separately. When reheating stuffing, heat only amount needed.

Opposite: Chicken Normandy, page 94.

BAKED CHICKEN PARMESAN

6 slices dry bread
¼ cup parsley sprigs
½ cup cubed Parmesan
  cheese
2 teaspoons salt
1 cup melted butter or
  margarine

1 clove garlic, crushed
2 teaspoons Dijon-style
  mustard
1 teaspoon Worcestershire
  sauce
2 broiler-fryers (2½ to 3
  pounds each), cut up

Heat oven to 350° F. Break two slices bread into blender container. Cover; blend at medium speed until crumbed. Empty into shallow pan. Repeat process with remaining bread slices, leaving crumbs from last two slices in blender container. Add parsley. Cover; blend at medium speed until chopped. While blender is still running, tip center cap and gradually add cheese, blending until grated. Add mixture to crumbs in shallow pan. Add salt; mix well. Combine melted butter, garlic, mustard, and Worcestershire; cool. Dip chicken pieces into butter mixture; roll in crumb-cheese mixture. Place pieces in single layer in large, shallow baking pan. Bake about 1 hour or until chicken is tender, basting occasionally with pan drippings. *Makes 8 servings.*

ROAST CHICKEN WITH VEGETABLE STUFFING

4 slices bread
1 medium carrot, pared and
  cut up
2 stalks celery, cut up
1 medium onion, cut up
¼ cup parsley sprigs

⅓ cup butter or margarine
2 teaspoons salt
2 teaspoons dried tarragon
1 teaspoon dried thyme
1 roasting chicken (about 4
  pounds)

Heat oven to 375° F. Tear two slices bread into blender container. Cover; ◼blend at medium speed until coarsely crumbed. Empty into mixing bowl. Repeat process with remaining bread. Set aside. Put carrot, celery, onion, and parsley into blender container. Add water just to cover. Cover; blend at medium speed just until vegetables are chopped. Drain thoroughly in colander. Heat butter in large skillet. Add chopped vegetables, 1 teaspoon salt, tarragon, and thyme. Cook over medium heat, stirring occasionally, for 3 minutes or until vegetables are soft. Add vegetable mixture to bread crumbs; mix well. Sprinkle neck and body cavities of chicken with remaining 1 teaspoon salt. Stuff chicken loosely with vegetable-crumb mixture. (Put any leftover stuffing into covered casserole or wrap in foil. Bake in oven with chicken during last 15 minutes of roasting.) Truss chicken; place in roasting pan, breast side up. Roast about 2 hours or until golden brown and fork-tender. *Makes 4 to 6 servings.*

93

TWIN BRAISED CHICKENS WITH CASHEW-RICE STUFFING

1 cup cashew nuts	2 cups cooked rice
3 tablespoons melted butter or margarine	2 whole broiler-fryers (about 2½ pounds each)
7 tablespoons dry white wine	All-purpose flour
	Salt and pepper
1 clove garlic, halved	¼ cup butter or margarine
1 small onion, cut up	1 cup chicken broth, or 1
2 stalks celery, cut up	chicken bouillon cube
4 sprigs parsley	dissolved in 1 cup hot
½ teaspoon salt	water
¼ teaspoon pepper	All-purpose flour
½ teaspoon dried thyme	(optional)

Put nuts into blender container. Cover; ◖ blend at

medium speed until chopped. Empty into mixing bowl. Put melted butter, 3 tablespoons wine, and garlic into blender container. Cover; blend at high speed until garlic is liquefied. Add onion, celery, and parsley. Cover; blend at medium speed just until vegetables are chopped. Add to chopped nuts; add seasonings and rice; toss lightly. Stuff chickens loosely with rice mixture; truss; dust with flour seasoned with salt and pepper. Heat ¼ cup butter in Dutch oven. Add chickens; cook until well browned. Add chicken broth and remaining wine. Cover; simmer 30 to 40 minutes or until chickens are tender, basting occasionally with liquid in pan. Remove chickens to heated serving platter. Thicken gravy with flour if desired. *Makes 6 servings.*

CHICKEN NORMANDY

¼ cup butter or margarine	8 sprigs parsley
2 broiler-fryers (1½ to 2 pounds each), cut up	⅓ cup dry sherry
¼ cup brandy	1 teaspoon salt
1 medium onion, cut up	¼ teaspoon pepper
2 stalks celery, cut up	¼ cup heavy cream
2 tart apples, pared, quartered, and cored	Apple wedges (optional)
	Parsley sprig (optional)

Heat butter in large skillet. Add chicken pieces; cook until well browned. Pour brandy over chicken; ignite. When flame burns out, remove chicken, leaving pan drippings in skillet. Put onion, celery, apples, and parsley into blender container; add water to cover. Cover; blend at low speed just until vegetables and apples are chopped. Drain well in colander. Empty into skillet with pan drippings;

cook about 5 minutes, stirring occasionally. Add sherry, salt, and pepper. Return chicken to pan; spoon sauce over chicken. Cover; simmer 20 to 25 minutes or until chicken is tender. Stir in cream; heat to serving temperature. Garnish with apple wedges and parsley if desired. *Makes 4 to 6 servings*.

CHICKEN BREASTS SUPREME

3 whole chicken breasts, split and boned
Salt
8 tablespoons butter or margarine
½ cup chicken broth, or ½ chicken bouillon cube dissolved in ½ cup hot water

½ cup dry white wine
2 tablespoons all-purpose flour
¼ teaspoon salt
Dash pepper
¼ cup heavy cream

Sprinkle chicken breasts lightly with salt. Heat 6 tablespoons butter in large skillet. Add chicken breasts. Cook over medium heat about 4 minutes on each side or until done. Remove breasts to serving platter; keep warm. Put chicken broth, wine, remaining 2 tablespoons butter, flour, ¼ teaspoon salt, and pepper into blender container. Cover; blend at high speed until smooth. Pour into same skillet. Cook over low heat, stirring constantly, until mixture thickens and comes to a boil. Stir in cream; heat gently. Pour over chicken. *Makes 6 servings*.

Serving Suggestion: Serve with hot, cooked rice.

Ladies' Luncheon

Chicken Croquettes (page 97)   A La King Sauce (page 173)
Crisp Green Salad   Honey French Dressing (page 166)
Parker House Rolls (page 143)   Parsley Butter (page 46)
Coffee Charlotte Russe (page 190)
Coffee   Tea

CHICKEN CURRY

1⅓ cups flaked coconut
1⅓ cups scalded milk
1 medium onion, cut up
1 stalk celery, cut up
1 tart apple, pared, quartered, and cored
2 tablespoons butter or margarine
2 tablespoons all-purpose flour
1 tablespoon curry powder

1 teaspoon salt
½ teaspoon ground ginger
⅛ teaspoon pepper
1½ cups chicken broth, or 1½ chicken bouillon cubes dissolved in 1½ cups hot water
3 cups cubed cooked chicken
1 tablespoon lemon juice
½ cup heavy cream

Put coconut and scalded milk into blender container. Cover; blend at high speed until coconut is pulverized. Strain into small bowl through fine sieve or double-thick cheesecloth (you should have 1 cup coconut milk). Set aside. Put onion, celery, and apple into blender container; add water just to cover. Cover; blend at medium speed just until vegetables and apple are chopped. Drain thoroughly in colander. Heat butter in large skillet. Add onion, celery, and apple; cook over medium heat, stirring occasionally, for 5 minutes. Stir in flour, curry powder, salt, ginger, and pepper; cook over low heat, stirring constantly, for 3 minutes. Put contents of skillet and ½ cup chicken broth into blender container. Cover; blend at high speed until smooth. Return mixture to skillet; add remaining chicken broth and coconut milk. Cook, stirring, until mixture comes to a boil. Cover; simmer over low heat 20 minutes. Add chicken and lemon juice; cook until thoroughly heated. Just before serving, stir in cream; heat gently. *Makes 6 servings*.

Serving Suggestion: Serve over hot, cooked rice and accompany with curry condiments, such as chutney, salted peanuts, banana slices, grated coconut, and raisins.

CHICKEN A LA KING

1 medium green pepper,
seeded and cut up
1 canned pimiento, cut up
3 parsley sprigs
1 cup light cream
½ cup chicken broth, or ½
chicken bouillon cube
dissolved in ½ cup hot
water
3 tablespoons softened
butter or margarine

3 tablespoons all-purpose
flour
¼ teaspoon salt
Dash pepper
2 cups cubed cooked
chicken
2 tablespoons dry sherry
(optional)

Put green pepper, pimiento, and parsley into
blender container. Cover; blend at medium speed
until chopped. Add cream, chicken broth, butter,
flour, salt, and pepper. Cover; blend at medium
speed until smooth. Pour into saucepan; heat to
simmering. Add chicken; heat through. If desired,
stir in sherry and heat gently. *Makes 4 servings*.

Serving Suggestion: Serve over hot, cooked rice
or toast points.

Turkey or Tuna à la King: Substitute 2 cups
cubed cooked turkey, or two cans (6½ or 7 ounces
each) tuna, drained and flaked, for chicken.
Proceed as for Chicken à la King.

CHICKEN CROQUETTES

2 cups cubed cooked
chicken
1 cup milk
¼ cup softened butter or
margarine
⅓ cup all-purpose flour
½ teaspoon salt
¼ teaspoon pepper

⅛ teaspoon poultry seasoning
1 stalk celery, cut up
1 small onion, cut up
6 slices dry bread
2 eggs
Vegetable oil for
deep-frying

Put a few cubes chicken into blender container.
Cover; blend at medium speed until ground. While

blender is still running, tip center cap and add 1 cup chicken cubes, blending until ground; empty into mixing bowl. Repeat process with remaining chicken. Put milk, butter, flour, salt, pepper, poultry seasoning, celery, and onion into blender container. Cover; blend at high speed until smooth. Pour into saucepan; cook over low heat, stirring constantly, until mixture thickens and comes to a boil. Add to chicken; mix well. Chill several hours. Break two slices bread into blender container. Cover; blend at medium speed until crumbed. Empty into pie plate. Repeat process with remaining bread, two slices at a time; empty into pie plate. Beat eggs lightly in shallow bowl. Shape chicken mixture into twelve ovals or cones. Roll in crumbs, then in beaten egg and again in crumbs, coating thoroughly. Chill for 30 minutes. Heat 1½-inch depth of oil in skillet or deep, heavy saucepan to 275° F. on deep-fat thermometer. Fry croquettes about 3 minutes or until golden brown; drain on paper towels. *Makes 6 servings.*

98

BAKED TURKEY HASH

2 cups cubed cooked turkey	1 canned pimiento, cut up
2 carrots, pared and cut up	8 parsley sprigs
1 medium onion, cut up	½ teaspoon salt
1 medium potato, pared and cut up	½ teaspoon thyme
	2 cans (10½ ounces each) turkey gravy

Heat oven to 350° F. Put a few cubes turkey into blender container. Cover; blend at medium speed until finely chopped. While blender is still running, tip center cap and gradually add 1 cup turkey cubes, blending until chopped; empty into mixing bowl. Repeat process with remaining turkey. Put carrots, onion, potato, pimiento, and parsley into blender container. Add water to cover. Cover; blend at medium speed just until vegetables are chopped. Drain thoroughly in colander. Add vegetables, salt, thyme, and turkey gravy to turkey; mix thoroughly. Turn into 1½-quart casserole; cover. Bake 45 minutes. Uncover. Bake about 15 minutes longer or until browned on top. *Makes 4 servings*.

ROAST DUCKLING WITH APPLE-PRUNE STUFFING

12 slices bread	¼ cup melted butter or
2 large tart apples, pared, quartered, and cored	margarine
	½ teaspoon salt
1 cup stewed pitted prunes	½ teaspoon dried marjoram
2 tablespoons liquid from prunes	½ teaspoon dried thyme
	1 duckling (5 to 6 pounds)

Heat oven to 325° F. Tear two slices bread into blender container. Cover; ⊓ blend at medium speed until coarsely crumbed. Empty into mixing bowl. Repeat process with remaining bread. Cut apple quarters into thirds. Put pieces into blender container. Add water to cover. Cover; blend at medium speed just until apples are chopped. Drain thoroughly in colander. Put remaining ingredients except duckling into blender container in order listed. Cover; blend at medium speed just until prunes are chopped. Add to bread crumbs; add apples; mix well. Stuff duckling loosely with apple-prune mixture; truss. Insert meat thermometer in thickest part of duckling between breast and thigh. Place duckling, breast side up, on rack in shallow roasting pan. Roast about 2½ hours or until meat thermometer registers 190° F. *Makes 4 servings*.

To Crisp Duckling: For crisp-skinned duckling and well-done meat, increase oven heat to 425° F. for last 15 minutes of roasting.

Fish and Shellfish

Much like poultry, fish is high in protein and most is low in fat, making it a suitable choice for dieters and calorie counters. It is especially good for those people who have a high cholesterol level. Iodine, B vitamins, and some calcium (if the bone is left in) are also found in fish and shellfish.

As for discovering some of the succulent ways fish can be prepared, you need only browse through this book. You'll find that the blender can do a superb job of either blending the fish, as in Whitefish Quenelles, or in making the subtly flavored Sauce Normande (page 174) to be served with it. The Baked Stuffed Red Snapper is a fisherman's delight, especially with its blender-chopped mushroom-vegetable stuffing seasoned with herbs. Equally good is the Poached Fillets in Herb-Wine Sauce, with its built-in tarragon sauce.

Secrets to Fish and Shellfish Cookery

The sooner fresh fish is used, the more flavorful it will be; it will also have a better texture. However, if you do not plan to use it immediately, wipe it with a damp cloth, wrap it in plastic wrap or aluminum foil or place it in a tightly covered container, and store it in the refrigerator.

Handle fish delicately and as little as possible during and after cooking. Fish to be fried should be dried thoroughly to prevent spattering.

Baste lean fish with melted butter or margarine while broiling or baking.

Do not overcook any fish or shellfish. Fish is done when it has a creamy color, can be easily pierced with a fork, and flakes when separated; it should, however, still be juicy.

Do not allow boiled shrimp, such as those being prepared for shrimp cocktails, to stand in hot water after they have been cooked—they will continue to cook and toughen.

Opposite: Fried Shrimp in Beer Batter, page 109.

BAKED STUFFED RED SNAPPER

1 red snapper (about 4
    pounds)
2 slices bread
8 parsley sprigs
2 large onions, cut up
2 carrots, pared and cut up
2 stalks celery, cut up
4 tablespoons butter or
    margarine
½ pound mushrooms
2 green onions, white parts
    only, cut up

1 tablespoon lemon juice
1 can (16 ounces) tomatoes,
    drained
½ teaspoon dried thyme
1 teaspoon salt
⅛ teaspoon pepper
¼ cup melted butter or
    margarine
Salt and pepper

Remove backbone from fish (or have market man do
it); leave head on or remove it (fish will be juicier if
baked with head on). Tear bread slices into blender
container; add parsley. Cover; blend at medium
speed until bread is crumbed and parsley is
chopped. Empty onto wax paper; set aside. Put
onions, carrots, and celery into blender container.
Add water to cover. Cover; blend at medium speed
just until chopped. Drain thoroughly in colander.
Heat 2 tablespoons butter in large skillet. Add
chopped vegetables; cook over medium heat,
stirring occasionally, 10 to 15 minutes. Place in
shallow baking pan. Heat oven to 425° F. Wipe
mushrooms with damp cloth; cut up; put into
blender container. Add green onions. Cover; blend
at medium speed until chopped. Heat remaining 2
tablespoons butter in skillet. Add green onions and
mushrooms; sprinkle with lemon juice; cook over
medium heat, stirring occasionally, 5 minutes. Put

tomatoes, thyme, 1 teaspoon salt, and ⅛ teaspoon pepper into blender container. Cover; blend at medium speed until tomatoes are chopped. Add to vegetables in skillet; simmer 10 minutes. Remove from heat; stir in bread crumb mixture. Stuff fish loosely with crumb mixture. Skewer or sew closed; place on vegetables in baking pan. Brush with melted butter; sprinkle with salt and pepper. Bake 30 to 35 minutes, allowing about 8 minutes per pound, basting often with pan juice. *Makes 8 servings.*

Note: Striped bass or bluefish may be used in place of red snapper.

OVEN-FRIED FISH FILLETS

6 slices dry bread	2 pounds fish fillets
1 tablespoon paprika	2 tablespoons melted butter
1 cup milk	or margarine
2 teaspoons salt	

Heat oven to 425° F. Break two slices bread into blender container. Cover; blend at medium speed until crumbed. Empty into shallow dish. Repeat process with remaining bread slices. Stir in paprika. Combine milk and salt in second shallow dish. Dip fillets into milk mixture, then into bread crumb mixture, coating them well. Place in lightly greased, shallow baking pan; drizzle lightly with melted butter. Bake 12 to 15 minutes or until fish is browned and crisp. *Makes 6 servings.*

Open House Buffet
Celery Stuffed with Roquefort Cheese Spread (page 38)
Cheddar and Port Wine Spread (page 38)   Crackers
Fried Shrimp in Beer Batter (page 109)
Swedish Meatballs (page 80)
Curried Deviled Eggs (page 40)
Beef Stroganoff (page 76)   Fluffy Rice
Key Lime Tarts (page 217)
Coffee

POACHED FILLETS IN HERB-WINE SAUCE

1½ to 2 pounds fillets of sole, flounder, or perch

3 green onions, white parts only, or ½ small onion, cut up

1 small clove garlic, halved

2 tablespoons all-purpose flour

1 cup dry white wine

2 tablespoons melted butter or margarine

6 sprigs parsley

½ teaspoon dried tarragon

¼ cup light cream

Heat oven to 350° F. Arrange fillets in large, lightly greased, shallow baking dish. Put remaining ingredients into blender container in order listed. Cover; blend at high speed until well mixed. Pour over fillets. Bake 30 minutes or until fish flakes easily, basting frequently with sauce in pan. *Makes 4 to 6 servings.*

POACHED SALMON STEAKS WITH SAUCE VERTE
(Green Mayonnaise)

4 salmon steaks (¾ pound each)

1 medium onion, cut up

2 cups boiling water

1 cup dry white wine

2 parsley sprigs

1 bay leaf

1 teaspoon salt

Sauce Verte (page 181)

Wrap each salmon steak in double thickness of

cheesecloth; set aside. Put onion into blender container. Cover; blend at medium speed until chopped. Put onion, water, wine, parsley, bay leaf, and salt in large skillet. Arrange salmon steaks in skillet. Simmer 15 to 20 minutes. To serve hot, remove from liquid immediately with broad spatula; remove cheesecloth. To serve cold, allow salmon steaks to cool in liquid (it helps keep them moist); remove from liquid; remove cheesecloth. Serve hot or cold with Sauce Verte. *Makes 4 servings*.

GEFILTE FISH

3 pounds mixed fish (1
    pound each whitefish,
    pike, and carp)
1 quart water
1 medium onion
2 stalks celery, cut up
2 carrots, pared and cut up
3 teaspoons salt

1 medium onion, cut up
1 cup cold water
2 eggs
4 slices dry bread or ¼ cup
    matzo meal
1 teaspoon salt
¼ teaspoon pepper

Remove heads from fish; skin and bone fish; cut fish into 1-inch cubes (or have market man do all this for you). Put heads, skin, and bones into large saucepan. Add 1 quart water, whole onion, celery, carrot, and 2 teaspoons salt. Bring to a boil; lower heat; simmer 30 minutes. Put 1 cup cubed fish and cut-up onion into blender container. Cover; blend at medium speed until finely chopped. If necessary, stop blender during processing and push ingredients toward blades with rubber spatula. Empty into large mixing bowl. Put ½ cup cold water, eggs, two slices bread torn into pieces or half the matzo meal, and half the remaining cubed fish into blender container. Cover; blend at medium speed until almost smooth. Add to fish in mixing bowl. Repeat with remaining water, bread or matzo meal, and cubed fish; add remaining salt and the pepper. Mix ingredients in bowl thoroughly. Wet hands; shape mixture loosely into balls, each about the size of an egg. Strain fish stock; remove and reserve carrots; discard other vegetables. Return stock to saucepan; bring to a boil. Add fish balls to boiling stock; reduce heat; simmer 1½ hours. Cool. Remove fish balls from stock with slotted spoon; chill. Strain stock; chill until jelled. Slice reserved carrots for garnish. Serve with jellied stock. *Makes 10 servings*.

Serving Suggestion: Serve with prepared horseradish.

WHITEFISH QUENELLES

1½ pounds fillet of pike or other white-fleshed fish, cut into ½-inch strips
½ teaspoon salt

1 egg white
1 ice cube, cracked
1 cup heavy cream

Put fish, salt, egg white, and ice cube into blender container. Cover; blend at high speed until smooth. If necessary, stop blender during processing and push ingredients toward blades with rubber spatula. While blender is running, tip center cap and gradually add cream. Blend until mixture is smooth, creamy, and thick. Chill. Heat 1-inch depth of lightly salted water to simmering in large skillet. Drop fish mixture from two tablespoons into simmering water. Poach gently 8 to 10 minutes, basting constantly with liquid in pan. Remove quenelles with slotted spoon; place on clean towel to drain. *Makes 4 to 6 servings*.

Serving Suggestion: Serve with Sauce Normande (page 174).

FISH CAKES

2 slices dry bread
4 tablespoons butter or
 margarine
1 medium onion, sliced
⅓ cup milk
2 eggs

2 slices bread, torn into
 pieces
¾ teaspoon dry mustard
½ teaspoon salt
2 cups flaked cooked cod or
 other white fish

Break dry bread into blender container. Cover; blend at medium speed until crumbed. Empty onto wax paper; set aside. Heat 2 tablespoons butter in small skillet. Add onion. Cook over medium heat, stirring occasionally, until soft but not browned. Put onion and remaining ingredients except bread and 2 tablespoons butter into blender container in order listed. Cover; blend at high speed until smooth. Chill several hours. Shape mixture into ten to twelve cakes. Dust lightly with reserved bread crumbs. Heat remaining 2 tablespoons butter in large skillet. Add fish cakes. Cook over low heat about 4 minutes or until lightly browned on underside. Turn; brown second side. *Makes 5 to 6 servings.*

Patio Supper
Tuna Noodle Casserole (page 108)
Roman Zucchini (page 129)
Tossed Green Salad   French Dressing (page 165)
Bread Sticks
Apple Walnut Crisp (page 185)
Coffee

TUNA NOODLE CASSEROLE

2 cups coarsely broken corn
    chips
½ cup milk
½ cup mayonnaise
1 can (10¾ ounces)
    condensed cream of
    celery or mushroom soup
1 medium onion, cut up
½ medium green pepper,
    seeded and cut up

1 canned pimiento
½ teaspoon salt
    Dash hot pepper sauce
½ of 8-ounce package
    medium noodles, cooked
    and drained
2 cans (6½ or 7 ounces
    each) tuna, drained and
    flaked

Heat oven to 350° F. Put 1 cup corn chips into
blender container. Cover; ∎ blend at medium speed
until crumbed. Empty onto wax paper. Set aside.
Repeat process with remaining corn chips. Put
milk, mayonnaise, soup, onion, green pepper,
pimiento, salt, and hot pepper sauce into blender
container. Cover; blend at medium speed until
vegetables are chopped. Combine noodles, tuna,
and chopped vegetable mixture in large bowl; stir
gently until thoroughly mixed. Spoon half the
mixture into greased 2-quart casserole; sprinkle
with half the corn chip crumbs. Repeat layers. Bake
35 minutes or until bubbly. *Makes 4 to 6 servings.*

SCALLOPED OYSTERS

8 slices bread, toasted
¼ cup butter or margarine
2 dozen shucked oysters,
    drained
¼ cup oyster liquid
1 thin slice onion

2 tablespoons dry sherry
2 tablespoons light cream
1 teaspoon Worcestershire
    sauce
½ teaspoon salt
    Dash cayenne pepper

Heat oven to 425° F. Spread toast slices with butter.
Break two slices toast into blender container.

Cover; **⊓** blend at medium speed until coarsely crumbed. Empty onto wax paper. Set aside. Repeat process with remaining toast slices. Sprinkle one-third of the crumbs into greased shallow 1½-quart casserole. Arrange half the oysters over crumbs. Put oyster liquid and remaining ingredients into blender container in order listed. Cover; blend at medium speed until onion is finely chopped. Pour half the mixture over oysters. Sprinkle with one-third of the crumbs. Repeat with remaining oysters, liquid mixture, and crumbs. Bake, uncovered, 30 minutes. *Makes 4 to 6 servings.*

FRIED SHRIMP IN BEER BATTER

1 cup beer
2 eggs
2 tablespoons vegetable oil
1¼ cups all-purpose flour
1 teaspoon salt

Dash cayenne pepper
2 pounds shelled shrimp
Vegetable oil for
  deep-frying

Put beer, eggs, vegetable oil, flour, salt, and cayenne into blender container. Cover; blend at high speed until smooth. Let stand 5 minutes. Heat 3-inch depth of oil in deep, heavy pan to 365° F. on deep-fat thermometer. Dip shrimp into batter; let excess drip off. Add to hot oil a few at a time; fry until golden brown, turning once. Drain on paper towels. *Makes 6 servings.*

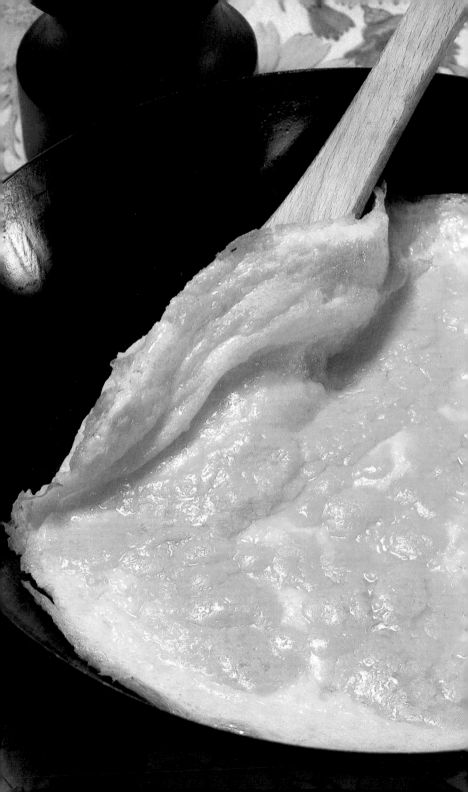

Eggs, Cheese, and Rice

Eggs are excellent as main dishes as well as in beverages and desserts, for they supply the basic protein essential for bodily growth and energy. In fact, nutritionists agree that after human breast milk, eggs provide the highest quality of protein available. In their general value to the body, they rank even higher than cow's milk, meat, or fish, for they are valuable sources of vitamins A, B, D, iron, and other important minerals. Fortunately, the variety of special egg dishes available to spark everyday menus is nearly limitless. If you do nothing more than browse through the ingredients lists of the recipes in this book, you will quickly discover how heavily we depend upon eggs to contribute to all meals—especially breakfast and brunch, lunch, and light suppers. And if you try some of these recipes, you will find that the blender can make serving a perfect food easier, quicker, and more exciting than you ever thought possible. As simple an entree as an omelet, in any one of its countless variations, can be a snap when prepared with the blender—and it'll be delicious, too. For more elegant occasions, the blender can help you prepare such delectable offerings as Company Scrambled Eggs, made hearty with a white sauce base.

The blender is equally useful in preparing cheese dishes, for most of them call for grating the cheese as a first step. Because cheese offers such a variety of flavors and textures, it is excellent in main dishes and appetizers of all descriptions as well as in sauces and as toppings for vegetable and other side dishes. As we all know, few dishes can rival a perfect cheese soufflé in delectableness, or fresh au gratin vegetables in flavor.

Rice is a cereal grain and is a good source of the B vitamins, calcium, and iron. Rice is also a nutritious budget-stretcher when combined with high-protein foods, such as eggs, cheese, and milk. Rice in its many cooked forms—from a plain side dish to a bed for curry to a broth-based pilaf to a dessert pudding or custard—is a mealtime standby.

111

Opposite: Cheese Omelet, page 114.

SCRAMBLED EGGS

¼ cup milk
4 eggs
½ teaspoon salt

1 tablespoon butter or
margarine

Put all ingredients except butter into blender container in order listed. Cover; blend at low speed just until mixed. Melt butter in skillet over low heat. Add egg mixture; cook slowly, stirring gently, until eggs are of desired consistency. *Makes 2 servings*.

Herb Scrambled Eggs: Start blender at medium speed. While blender is running, tip center cap and add ¼ cup parsley sprigs and 1 tablespoon cut-up fresh tarragon, chives, or basil leaves, blending until chopped. Proceed as for Scrambled Eggs. To prepare with dried herbs, add 1 teaspoon herb of your choice to blender container with eggs.

Cheese Scrambled Eggs: Start blender at medium speed. While blender is running, tip center cap and gradually add ½ cup cubed Cheddar or Swiss cheese, blending until grated. Proceed as for Scrambled Eggs.

112

COMPANY SCRAMBLED EGGS

1 cup milk
14 eggs
2 teaspoons salt
¼ teaspoon pepper

¼ cup butter or margarine
2 cups Medium White Sauce
(page 170)

Put milk, eggs, salt, and pepper into blender container. Cover; blend at low speed just until thoroughly mixed. Melt butter in large skillet over low heat. Add egg mixture; cook over low heat, stirring gently, until eggs begin to set. Stir in Medium White Sauce. Cook, stirring gently, until of desired consistency. *Makes 8 servings.*

Company Scrambled Eggs Fines Herbes: Start blender at medium speed. While blender is running, tip center cap and add ¾ cup parsley sprigs, 3 tablespoons cut-up fresh chives, and 3 tablespoons cut-up fresh tarragon or chervil; blend until chopped. Proceed as for Company Scrambled Eggs. To use dried herbs, add 1 tablespoon dried tarragon or chervil to blender container with eggs.

OMELET

3 eggs
1 tablespoon water
¼ teaspoon salt
  Dash pepper or few
    dashes hot pepper sauce

1 tablespoon butter or
  margarine

Put eggs, water, salt, and pepper into blender container. Cover; blend at low speed just until thoroughly mixed. Heat omelet pan; add butter; swirl around in pan to coat bottom and sides. Pour egg mixture into pan; stir rapidly with fork until eggs just begin to set. Tilt pan, lifting set edge of eggs with spatula to allow uncooked eggs to run to bottom of pan. Shake skillet occasionally to keep omelet moving freely in pan. Cook until omelet is set but still moist on top. Tilt skillet; fold omelet with spatula; turn out onto serving plate. *Makes 1 serving.*

Herb Omelet: Start blender at medium speed. While blender is running, tip center cap and add 2 tablespoons cut-up parsley sprigs or 1 tablespoon cut-up fresh tarragon, chives, chervil, or basil leaves, blending until chopped. Proceed as for Omelet.

Cheese Omelet: Prepare 2 tablespoons grated Swiss or Cheddar cheese (page 16); set aside. Proceed as for Omelet. Sprinkle with grated cheese before folding.

Western Omelet: Put Omelet ingredients except water into blender container. Add ¼ cup diced cooked ham, two strips green pepper, one slice onion, and one slice tomato. Cover; blend at medium speed until green pepper and onion are chopped. Proceed as for Omelet.

Spanish Omelet: Prepare Omelet as above. Before folding, spoon 3 tablespoons Spanish Sauce (page 179) over omelet. Fold omelet; turn out onto serving plate. Serve with additional Spanish Sauce.

Holiday Family Buffet Breakfast

Fresh Apple Juice (page 52)
Company Scrambled Eggs (page 112)
Canadian Bacon
Date-Nut Muffins (page 136)   Sour Cream Coffee Cake (page 139)
Cheese Buns (page 145)
Coffee   Tea

CHEESE SOUFFLE

1 cup cubed sharp Cheddar cheese	¼ teaspoon dry mustard
¼ cup butter or margarine	⅛ teaspoon pepper
¼ cup all-purpose flour	⅛ teaspoon ground nutmeg
½ teaspoon salt	1 cup hot milk
	4 eggs, separated

Heat oven to 375° F. Put cheese, butter, flour, salt, mustard, pepper, and nutmeg into blender container. Add hot milk and egg yolks. Cover; blend at high speed until smooth. Pour into saucepan.

Cook over low heat, stirring constantly, until sauce is thick and smooth. Remove from heat; cool. Beat egg whites with electric mixer until stiff but not dry. Stir about ½ cup beaten egg whites into cheese sauce to lighten it. Fold in remaining egg whites. Turn into ungreased 1½-quart soufflé dish. Smooth surface with spatula. Bake 35 to 40 minutes or until soufflé is puffed and golden brown. Serve at once. *Makes 4 servings.*

Spinach Soufflé: Cook 1 package (10 ounces) frozen chopped spinach according to package directions. Drain thoroughly, squeezing as much moisture as possible from spinach. Prepare sauce for Cheese Soufflé, omitting cheese. Stir spinach into sauce. Proceed as for Cheese Soufflé.

CHEESE FONDUE

115

1⅓ cups dry white wine	Dash pepper
¾ pound Swiss or Gruyère cheese, cubed	Dash paprika
1 small clove garlic, halved	3 tablespoons kirsch
½ teaspoon salt	1 tablespoon cornstarch
Dash ground nutmeg	1 loaf French bread, cubed

Heat wine in medium saucepan; do not boil. Put cheese, garlic, salt, nutmeg, pepper, and paprika into blender container. Add heated wine. Cover; blend at medium speed until smooth. Mix kirsch with cornstarch until smooth. Add to cheese mixture. Cover; blend at medium speed until thoroughly mixed. Pour into saucepan; heat gently. Serve in fondue dish or casserole over candle warmer. To eat, spear a cube of bread with long-handled fork and dip into fondue. *Makes 4 to 6 servings.*

QUICHE LORRAINE

9-inch Unbaked Pastry
    Crust (page 212)
6 slices bacon
1 onion, thinly sliced
1½ cups cubed Swiss or
    Gruyère cheese

4 eggs
2 cups light cream
½ teaspoon salt
⅛ teaspoon pepper
⅛ teaspoon ground nutmeg

Heat oven to 450° F. Bake pastry crust 5 minutes; remove from oven; cool. Cook bacon in skillet until crisp; drain; crumble; reserve. Pour off all but 1 tablespoon fat from skillet; add onion; cook over medium heat, stirring occasionally, until transparent. Start blender at medium speed. While blender is running, tip center cap and add ½ cup cheese cubes. Cover; blend at medium speed until grated. Empty onto wax paper. Repeat process with remaining cheese, ½ cup at a time. Put onion into pastry crust; sprinkle with bacon and cheese. Put eggs, cream, and seasonings into blender container. Cover; blend at low speed until thoroughly mixed. Pour into pastry crust. Bake 15 minutes. Reduce oven heat to 350° F. Bake 10 to 15 minutes or until thin-bladed knife inserted halfway between center and edge comes out clean. Let stand 10 minutes before cutting. Cut into wedges to serve. *Makes 12 appetizer or 6 main-dish servings.*

PILAF

1 large onion, cut up
¼ cup butter or margarine
1 cup long-grain rice

3 cups chicken or beef
    broth, or 3 chicken or
    beef bouillon cubes
    dissolved in 3 cups hot
    water

Put onion into blender container. Cover; blend at medium speed until chopped. Heat butter in large skillet. Add onion; cook over medium heat, stirring occasionally, until soft. Add rice; cook, stirring constantly, until rice starts to brown. Stir in broth. Simmer, covered, about 20 minutes or until rice is tender and all liquid is absorbed. *Makes 4 to 6 servings*.

Mushroom Pilaf: Wipe from eight to ten medium mushrooms with damp cloth; remove and discard stem ends. Start blender at medium speed. Tip center cap and add mushrooms, a few at a time, blending just until coarsely chopped. Cook with onions in Pilaf. Proceed as for Pilaf.

Almond Pilaf: Put ½ cup blanched almonds into blender container. Cover; blend at medium speed just until coarsely chopped. Empty onto wax paper; set aside. Proceed as for Pilaf; sprinkle with almonds before serving.

FRIED RICE

2 eggs
¼ cup vegetable oil
¼ pound mushrooms
1 cup cubed cooked ham
3 green onions, white parts
   only, cut up

4 cups cold cooked rice
2 tablespoons soy sauce
½ teaspoon sugar

Put eggs into blender container. Cover; blend at low speed until mixed. Heat 1 tablespoon oil in skillet. Add eggs; cook until firm. Remove to plate; cut into thin strips; set aside. Wipe mushrooms with a damp cloth and put into blender container with ham and onions. Cover; ◨ blend at medium speed until chopped. Heat remaining 3 tablespoons oil in skillet. Add ham, onions, and mushrooms. Cook over medium heat, stirring occasionally, until onion is tender-crisp. Add rice; cook, stirring constantly, until rice is well coated with oil and heated through. Add soy sauce and sugar; mix well. Stir in egg strips. *Makes 4 servings*.

Vegetables

Good nutrition abounds in the world of vegetable cookery. In general, vegetables are a source of vitamins A and C and of important minerals—iron and calcium. Dry vegetables, such as peas, beans, and lentils, supply protein as well as B vitamins and other nutrients. Vegetables are a boon to weight-watchers, for they are a low-calorie food that is pleasant to eat.

Secrets to Vegetable Cookery

Prepare vegetables immediately before cooking; cook them quickly and serve them promptly to retain maximum flavor and nutritive value.

Discover the variety of ways vegetables can be cooked:

Boil them in ½ to 1 inch of boiling, salted water until tender-crisp.

Steam them in a steamer basket set over rapidly boiling water just until tender-crisp. (They may also be steamed in a small amount of water in a covered casserole set in a 350° F. oven. Cooked in this way, vegetables take about two to three times longer than boiling.)

Bake them on the oven rack on a baking sheet or in a shallow casserole.

Braise them in a covered skillet or saucepan with about 2 tablespoons butter, margarine, or drippings and 1 or 2 tablespoons water. Cooked in this way, vegetables are also known as "panned."

Broil tender, raw vegetables, such as tomatoes and mushrooms, brushed with butter or margarine.

Fry or *stir-fry* them in a small amount of fat over medium heat or *French-fry* them in hot, deep fat.

Pressure cook or steam them under pressure, following manufacturer's directions.

119

Opposite: Asparagus Polonaise, page 120.

ASPARAGUS POLONAISE

1 hard-cooked egg, shelled
¼ cup parsley sprigs
2 slices dry bread
¼ cup butter or margarine

2 pounds asparagus or 2
packages (10 ounces
each) frozen asparagus,
cooked, drained, and
kept hot

Start blender at medium speed. While blender is running, tip center cap and add egg, blending until chopped. Empty into small bowl. Start blender at medium speed. While blender is running, tip center cap and add parsley, blending until chopped. Stir into chopped egg. Break bread into blender container. Cover; ⋈ blend at medium speed until crumbed. Heat butter in small skillet. Add bread crumbs; cook over medium heat, stirring occasionally, until golden brown. Combine with egg mixture; sprinkle over asparagus. *Makes 4 to 6 servings.*

Note: Crumb topping may also be used with broccoli or cauliflower.

BROCCOLI AU GRATIN

1 slice dry bread, buttered
½ cup cubed Swiss cheese
1 cup Medium White Sauce
(page 170)

1 bunch broccoli or 2
packages (10 ounces
each) frozen broccoli,
cooked and drained

Break bread into blender container. Cover; ⋈ blend at medium speed until crumbed. Empty onto wax paper; set aside. Start blender at medium speed. While blender is running, tip center cap and gradually add cheese, blending until grated. Empty onto another sheet of wax paper; set aside. Prepare

Medium White Sauce. Heat oven to 375° F. Put half the broccoli into buttered 1-quart baking dish. Add half the sauce; sprinkle with half the Swiss cheese. Repeat layers. Sprinkle top with bread crumbs. Bake 15 to 20 minutes or until bubbly and golden brown. *Makes 4 servings*.

Note: Asparagus or cauliflowerets may be used in place of broccoli. Cheddar cheese may be substituted for Swiss cheese. If desired, grated Parmesan cheese may be mixed with bread crumbs for topping.

GREEN BEANS VINAIGRETTE

¾ cup vegetable or olive oil
¼ cup lemon juice or red wine vinegar
½ teaspoon dry mustard
½ teaspoon salt
  Dash pepper
6 parsley sprigs
1 tablespoon cut-up fresh chervil leaves or 1 teaspoon dried chervil
1 tablespoon cut-up fresh chive
½ canned pimiento, cut up
1 pound fresh green beans or 2 packages (10 ounces each) frozen green beans, cooked and drained

Put all ingredients except green beans into blender container in order listed. Cover; blend at medium speed until herbs and pimiento are chopped. Pour into small saucepan; heat to lukewarm. Pour over green beans. Serve hot or let stand 1 hour, stirring once or twice, and serve. *Makes 4 servings*.

Asparagus Vinaigrette: Substitute cooked asparagus for green beans. Proceed as for Green Beans Vinaigrette.

ORANGE-GLAZED BEETS

3 tablespoons butter or margarine	2 tablespoons sugar
½ small onion, sliced	1 tablespoon cornstarch
1½ cups orange juice	½ teaspoon salt
1 thin slice orange	2 cans (1 pound each) sliced beets, drained
1 thin slice lemon	

Heat butter in saucepan. Add onion; cook over medium heat, stirring occasionally, until transparent. Put orange juice, orange and lemon slices, sugar, cornstarch, and salt into blender container. Add onion and butter mixture. Cover; blend at medium speed until orange and lemon slices are finely chopped. Return to saucepan. Simmer, stirring, until sauce thickens. Add beets; simmer, covered, 10 minutes. *Makes 6 to 8 servings.*

122

CREAMED CABBAGE

1 medium head green cabbage, coarsely cut up	2 tablespoons all-purpose flour
1 thin slice onion	1 teaspoon salt
¼ cup milk	⅛ teaspoon pepper
2 tablespoons softened butter or margarine	¼ teaspoon caraway seeds (optional)

Fill blender container to the 5-cup mark with cabbage. Add water just to cover cabbage. Cover; blend at medium speed until coarsely chopped. Drain thoroughly in colander; empty into saucepan. Repeat process with remaining cabbage. Put remaining ingredients except caraway seeds into blender container in order listed. Cover; blend at high speed until smooth. Add to cabbage; mix thoroughly. Cook over low heat, stirring frequently, 10 to 12 minutes or until cabbage is just tender.

Sprinkle with caraway seeds if desired. *Makes 6 servings*.

SWEET AND SOUR RED CABBAGE

1 medium head red
    cabbage, coarsely cut up
1 apple, quartered and
    cored

1 medium onion, cut up
⅓ cup sugar
1 cup water
½ cup red wine vinegar

Fill blender container up to 5-cup mark with cabbage, apple, and onion; add water just to cover. Cover; blend at medium speed until cabbage is coarsely chopped. Drain thoroughly in colander; empty into saucepan. Repeat process until all cabbage, apple, and onion are chopped. Add sugar, water, and vinegar. Cover; simmer 1 hour, stirring occasionally. *Makes 4 servings*.

123

BAKED CARROT RING

2½ cups pared carrots, sliced
    ½ inch thick
1 thin slice onion
3 eggs
1 cup light cream or
    half-and-half

3 tablespoons softened
    butter or margarine
2 tablespoons all-purpose
    flour
½ teaspoon salt
¼ teaspoon pepper

Heat oven to 350° F. Cook carrots and onion, covered, in 1-inch depth of boiling, salted water 12 to 15 minutes or until carrots are tender. Drain thoroughly. Put eggs, cream, butter, flour, salt, and pepper into blender container. Cover; blend at high speed until smooth. Add cooked carrots and onion. Cover; blend at low speed until smooth. Pour into greased 5-cup ring mold. Set mold in baking pan;

pour hot water into baking pan to depth of 1 inch. Bake 45 minutes or until thin-bladed knife inserted in center comes out clean. Remove from oven; let stand 5 minutes. Unmold onto serving plate. *Makes 6 to 8 servings.*

New Year's Day Buffet
Onion Soup (page 64)
Virginia Ham with Honey-Orange Glaze (page 183)
Creamed Cabbage (page 122)
Baked Orange Sweet Potatoes (page 127)
Pan Rolls (page 143)
Pecan Pie (page 215)
Coffee

CORN PUDDING

1 can (13 ounces) evaporated milk
¼ cup water
3 soda crackers, broken
3 eggs
1 can (16 ounces) cream-style corn
1 small onion, cut up
½ small green pepper, seeded and cut up
2 tablespoons butter or margarine
1 teaspoon salt
¼ teaspoon pepper
Paprika

Heat oven to 350° F. Heat evaporated milk and water to scalding. Put remaining ingredients except paprika into blender container in order listed. Add hot milk mixture. Cover; blend at medium speed until onion and green pepper are chopped and mixture is combined. Turn into greased 1½-quart baking dish; sprinkle with paprika. Set dish in larger pan; pour hot water into larger pan to depth of 1 inch. Bake 1 hour 20 minutes or until thin-bladed knife inserted in center comes out clean. *Makes 6 to 8 servings.*

CHEESE-BAKED ONIONS

4 slices dry bread, buttered
½ cup cubed Swiss cheese
2 cups Thin White Sauce
(page 171)

2 pounds small white
onions, peeled, cooked,
and drained

Heat oven to 400° F. Break two slices bread into blender container. Cover; ◖ blend at medium speed until crumbed. Empty into bowl. Repeat process with remaining bread. Start blender at medium speed. While blender is running, tip center cap and gradually add cheese, blending until grated. Stir into bread crumbs. Prepare Thin White Sauce. Put onions into greased 1½-quart baking dish. Pour sauce over onions. Sprinkle with crumb mixture. Bake 15 minutes or until bubbly and golden brown. *Makes 4 to 6 servings.*

125

DUCHESS POTATOES

Packaged instant mashed
potatoes for 6 servings
Boiling water
Milk
2 tablespoons butter or
margarine
½ teaspoon salt

⅛ teaspoon nutmeg
Dash cayenne pepper
1 egg
2 egg yolks
Melted butter or
margarine

Heat oven to 450° F. or heat broiler. Following package directions for instant mashed potatoes, put half the amount of water and entire amount of milk specified into blender container. Add butter, salt, nutmeg, and cayenne. Cover; blend at medium speed until mixed. While blender is running, tip center cap and add egg and egg yolks; add potatoes slowly; blend until smooth. Spoon in mounds or put through pastry tube onto greased cookie sheet. Brush with melted butter. Brown in oven or under broiler. *Makes 6 servings*.

SCALLOPED POTATOES

3 slices bread, buttered	1 teaspoon salt
1 small onion, cut up	¼ teaspoon pepper
6 medium potatoes, pared and thinly sliced	1¾ cups milk

Heat oven to 350° F. Tear half the bread slices into blender container. Cover; ◼ blend at medium speed until crumbed. Empty onto wax paper; set aside. Repeat process with remaining bread. Put onion into blender container. Cover; ◼ blend at medium speed until chopped. Put one-third of potatoes in greased 1½-quart casserole; sprinkle with salt, pepper, one-third of onion, and one-third of crumbs. Repeat layers twice, ending with crumbs. Pour milk carefully down side of casserole so that top crumb layer is not disturbed. Cover; bake 30 minutes. Uncover; bake 30 minutes longer. *Makes 6 servings*.

POTATO PANCAKES

2 eggs	¼ teaspoon all-purpose flour
½ small onion, cut up	2½ cups cubed, pared potatoes
¼ teaspoon baking powder	
1 teaspoon salt	

Put eggs, onion, baking powder, salt, flour, and 1

cup potatoes into blender container. Cover; blend at medium speed until potatoes are grated and ingredients are thoroughly combined. Add remaining potatoes. Cover; blend at medium speed several seconds or just until potatoes are grated. Pour small amounts onto heated, well-greased griddle or skillet. Fry until golden brown on both sides. *Makes 8 to 10 pancakes.*

Latkes (Potato Pancakes with Matzo Meal): Use only one egg and omit baking powder and flour in Potato Pancake recipe. Prepare recipe through processing of potatoes. Stir in 2 tablespoons matzo meal. Heat ½-inch depth of vegetable oil in skillet. Pour small amounts of batter into hot oil. Fry until golden brown on both sides. Drain on paper towels. Serve with Fresh Applesauce (page 186).

127

BAKED ORANGE SWEET POTATOES

2 cans (18 ounces each) sweet potatoes, drained	⅓ cup firmly packed brown sugar
¼ cup butter or margarine	¼ teaspoon salt
1 small unpeeled orange, cut up	Dash ground nutmeg
	Dash ground ginger

Heat oven to 350° F. Slice sweet potatoes into 9 x 9 x 2-inch baking dish. Put remaining ingredients into blender container in order listed. Cover; blend at medium speed until orange is finely chopped. If necessary, stop blender during processing and push ingredients toward blades with rubber spatula. Spoon over sweet potatoes. Bake 30 minutes. *Makes 6 servings.*

CRUSTY PECAN SQUASH

1 medium butternut squash, pared, seeded, and cut up
½ cup pecans
⅓ cup sugar
½ teaspoon ground cinnamon
2 tablespoons maple syrup

Cook squash in a small amount of boiling, salted water until tender; drain. Heat broiler. Put pecans into blender container. Cover; ⋈ blend at medium speed until chopped. Empty onto wax paper; set aside. Put squash, sugar, and cinnamon into blender container. Cover; blend at low speed until smooth. Turn into 1-quart greased heatproof casserole. Top with chopped pecans; drizzle with maple syrup. Place under broiler 3 to 5 minutes or until glazed and browned. *Makes 4 servings.*

128

CREAMED SPINACH

1 package (10 ounces) fresh spinach
1 thin slice onion
1 cup milk
3 tablespoons softened butter or margarine
3 tablespoons all-purpose flour
½ teaspoon salt
⅛ teaspoon pepper
⅛ teaspoon ground nutmeg

Wash spinach well; shake off excess water; pat dry. Remove coarse stems and discard; tear large leaves into pieces. Put all ingredients except spinach into blender container in order listed. Cover; blend at medium speed until onion is very finely chopped. While blender is running, tip center cap and gradually add spinach, blending until chopped. Turn into saucepan. Cook over low heat, stirring frequently, 5 to 7 minutes. *Makes 4 servings.*

TOMATOES PROVENÇAL

4 medium tomatoes
½ teaspoon salt
¼ teaspoon pepper
2 slices dry bread
2 tablespoons softened
    butter or margarine

½ clove garlic
¼ cup parsley sprigs
1 teaspoon Dijon-style
    mustard

Heat oven to 375° F. Cut tomatoes in half horizontally. Arrange halves, cut side up, in greased, shallow baking pan. Sprinkle with salt and pepper. Spread each slice of bread with 1 tablespoon butter. Break bread slices into blender container. Cover; blend at medium speed until crumbed. Add garlic, parsley, and mustard. Cover; blend at medium speed until parsley is chopped and mixture is combined. Sprinkle mixture over tomato halves. Bake 20 minutes. *Makes 4 servings.*

ROMAN ZUCCHINI

4 medium tomatoes, peeled,
    cored, and cut up
1 medium onion, cut up
½ green pepper, seeded and
    cut up
1 stalk celery, cut up

1 clove garlic, halved
½ teaspoon salt
6 small zucchini (about 1½
    pounds), sliced
2 tablespoons butter or
    margarine

Put tomatoes into blender container. Cover; blend at low speed until pureed. Add onion, green pepper, celery, garlic, and salt. Cover; blend at medium speed until vegetables are chopped. Empty into large skillet. Add zucchini and butter. Cover; simmer 10 to 15 minutes, stirring occasionally, until zucchini is tender. *Makes 6 servings.*

Breads—Quick, Yeast, and Other

Batters for pancakes can be made in an instant and poured right from the blender container onto the griddle. You can whip up popover batter, too, almost before you know it. As for coffee cakes, fruit and nut breads, and muffins, all the necessary chopping can be quickly done by the blender and the chopped ingredients then combined with the batter just as quickly. (Biscuits and dumplings are not recommended for blender preparation.) Most important, the batter for a good yeast bread can be mixed in a matter of seconds with your blender, and the kneading time can be shortened.

Breads are generally categorized as either "quick" breads or "yeast" breads. Coffee cakes, muffins, nut and fruit breads are among those we call quick, because the leavening agent—baking powder—makes them rise so fast. Pancakes, waffles, dumplings, fritters, and doughnuts are also called quick—all are ready to bake, steam, or fry as soon as they are mixed.

"Yeast" breads require more time as well as specific temperatures for their successful preparation. They need time for the yeast to feed on the starch of the dough and the salt and sugar that control the "gas" and the rising action. The water used to dissolve the yeast must be just the right temperature—warm enough to activate the yeast but cool enough not to kill it. The dough must also be allowed to "rise" at a specific temperature—one just warm enough to allow the yeast to multiply. And, of course, bread, like all oven-baked items, requires a particular baking temperature.

Secrets to Making Quick Breads

Avoid overmixing and overhandling. All doughs should be handled lightly; doughs to be rolled should be patted only enough to enable them to be turned out onto a lightly floured board for shaping.

Blend batter for muffins, pancakes, and similar

Opposite: Date-Nut Muffins, page 136.

recipes just until the flour is well dampened. Over-blending these batters may cause an uneven texture, resulting in a less tender product.

Secrets to Making Yeast Breads

Provide the proper temperatures throughout the entire preparation process: the temperature of the water for dissolving the yeast should be from 105° to 115° F.; the temperature for the dough to rise in should be 85° F.; the temperature for baking is provided by the recipe.

Always bake bread and rolls in a preheated oven. If you are making two loaves or two pans of rolls, place them on the center shelf in the oven with at least 2 inches of space between the pans to allow for heat circulation. If you are making more than two pans, stagger them over two shelves and separate them by at least 2 inches.

Test breads for doneness by tapping the bottom of the loaf with your knuckles. If a hollow sound results, the bread is probably baked through. Other clues are a well-browned crust and a slight shrinkage from the sides of the pan.

Always remove breads from pans immediately to prevent soggy crusts.

OLD-FASHIONED PANCAKES

1¾ cups milk	2 cups sifted all-purpose
2 eggs	flour
3 tablespoons vegetable oil	1 tablespoon baking powder
or melted butter or	1 teaspoon salt
margarine	

Put all ingredients into blender container in order listed. Cover; blend at high speed just until mixed. If necessary, stop blender during processing and push ingredients toward blades with rubber spatula.

Pour about ¼ cup batter onto lightly greased, preheated griddle. Bake until bubbles form on surface and edges are dry. Turn; bake second side until golden brown. *Makes 12 four-inch pancakes*.

Nut Pancakes: Add ½ cup walnuts or pecans to batter; blend just until nuts are chopped. Bake as for Old-Fashioned Pancakes.

Apple Pancakes: Peel, core, and cut up one small tart apple. Add to batter. Blend just until apple is chopped. Bake as for Old-Fashioned Pancakes.

Cornmeal Pancakes: Use 1 cup yellow cornmeal and 1 cup sifted all-purpose flour in place of 2 cups all-purpose flour. Proceed as for Old-Fashioned Pancakes.

WAFFLES

1 cup milk	1 tablespoon sugar
2 eggs	1½ cups sifted all-purpose
3 tablespoons vegetable oil	flour
or melted butter or	1 tablespoon baking powder
margarine	½ teaspoon salt

Put all ingredients into blender container in order listed. Cover; blend at high speed just until mixed. If necessary, stop blender during processing and push ingredients toward blades with rubber spatula. Bake in preheated waffle iron according to manufacturer's directions. *Makes 6 waffles*.

To make pancakes from a prepared mix, use the proportions recommended on the package. Put the liquid and eggs into the blender container; then add the pancake mix. Cover and blend at medium to high speed just until combined. Bake as directed.

FRITTERS

Vegetable oil for
  deep-frying
½ cup milk
1 egg
1 tablespoon vegetable oil

1 cup sifted all-purpose
  flour
1 teaspoon baking powder
½ teaspoon salt

Heat 1½-inch depth of oil in skillet or deep, heavy
saucepan to 375° F. on deep-fat thermometer. Put
remaining ingredients into blender container in
order listed. Cover; blend at high speed just until
mixed. If necessary, stop blender during processing
and push ingredients toward blades with rubber
spatula. Drop batter by large spoonfuls into hot fat.
Fry 3 to 5 minutes or until browned on all sides.
Drain on paper towels. *Makes 10 to 12 fritters.*

Serving Suggestion: Serve with maple syrup or
Fresh Applesauce (page 186).

Corn Fritters: Add 1 cup cooked or canned,
drained, whole-kernel corn to batter. Cover; blend 5
seconds. Fry as for Fritters.

POPOVERS

1 cup milk
2 eggs
1 tablespoon vegetable oil

1 cup sifted all-purpose
  flour
½ teaspoon salt

Have all ingredients at room temperature. Heat
oven to 400° F. Grease eight 5-ounce custard cups
thoroughly. Put all ingredients into blender
container in order listed. Cover; blend at high speed
until mixed. If necessary, stop blender during
processing and push ingredients toward blades with
rubber spatula. Fill custard cups half full. Place on
cookie sheet. Bake 40 minutes or until deep, golden

brown; do not open oven door while baking. Serve at once. *Makes 8 popovers*.

Note: If you prefer dry popovers, puncture top of each baked popover with tines of fork to allow steam to escape. Return to oven with heat turned off for 10 minutes.

Cheese Popovers: Place cubed Cheddar, Swiss, or Gruyère cheese in center of each filled custard cup. Bake as for Popovers.

OLD-FASHIONED DOUGHNUTS

1½ cups sifted all-purpose flour
2 teaspoons baking powder
½ teaspoon salt
½ teaspoon ground nutmeg
½ cup milk
1 egg
2 tablespoons melted shortening
½ cup sugar
Vegetable oil for deep-frying

Sift flour, baking powder, salt, and nutmeg into medium bowl; set aside. Put milk, egg, shortening, and sugar into blender container. Cover; blend at low speed until mixed. Add half the dry ingredients. Cover; blend at low speed just until mixed. Add remaining dry ingredients. Cover; blend at high speed just until combined. If necessary, stop blender during processing and push ingredients toward blades with rubber spatula. Turn out onto well-floured surface. Roll out ½ inch thick. Cut with floured doughnut cutter. Gather trimmings; roll out and cut until all are used. Heat 2 to 3-inch depth of oil in skillet or deep, heavy saucepan to 375° F. on deep-frying thermometer. Fry doughnuts, a few at a time, about 4 minutes or until golden brown on one side. Turn with slotted spoon; fry until second side is brown. Drain on paper towels. *Makes 12 doughnuts.*

Serving Suggestion: Serve plain or sprinkled with granulated or confectioners' sugar.

Whole Wheat Doughnuts: Substitute ¾ cup unsifted whole wheat flour for ¾ cup all-purpose flour and add it to blender container with second addition of dry ingredients. Proceed as for Old-Fashioned Doughnuts. *Makes 12 doughnuts.*

Chocolate Doughnuts: Omit nutmeg and add one square melted unsweetened chocolate, ½ teaspoon vanilla, and 2 tablespoons additional sugar to milk mixture in blender. Proceed as for Old-Fashioned Doughnuts. *Makes 12 doughnuts.*

Doughnut Puffs: Drop Old-Fashioned Doughnut batter by scant teaspoonfuls into hot fat; fry until golden. *Makes about 24 to 30 puffs.*

MUFFINS

2 cups sifted all-purpose flour	2 tablespoons sugar
2½ teaspoons baking powder	1 cup milk
½ teaspoon salt	1 egg
	½ cup soft shortening

Heat oven to 400° F. Grease twelve 2½-inch muffin-pan cups. Sift flour, baking powder, salt, and sugar into medium-size bowl. Put remaining ingredients into blender container in order listed. Cover; blend at low speed until well mixed. Pour over dry ingredients; stir just until moistened. Fill muffin cups two-thirds full. Bake 20 to 25 minutes or until done. *Makes 12 muffins.*

Date-Nut Muffins: Add ¾ cup pitted dates and ¼ cup walnuts to ingredients in blender container.

Cover; blend at low speed until dates and nuts are finely chopped. Proceed as for Muffins.

Raisin Muffins: Add 1 cup seedless raisins to ingredients in blender container. Cover; blend at low speed until raisins are finely chopped. Proceed as for Muffins.

Carrot Muffins: Add one carrot, pared and cut up, to ingredients in blender container. Cover; blend at low speed until carrot is finely chopped. Proceed as for Muffins.

Cranberry Muffins: Add 1 cup whole cranberries and ¼ cup sugar to ingredients in blender container. Cover; blend at low speed until cranberries are chopped. Proceed as for Muffins.

Blueberry Muffins: Prepare batter in Muffin recipe. Fold in 1 cup washed, fresh blueberries. Bake as for Muffins.

137

BRAN MUFFINS

1 cup sifted all-purpose flour	¼ cup molasses
2½ teaspoons baking powder	1 egg
1 teaspoon salt	1 cup all-bran cereal
3 tablespoons soft shortening	½ cup milk

Heat oven to 400° F. Grease twelve 2½-inch muffin-pan cups. Sift flour, baking powder, and salt into medium-size bowl. Put shortening, molasses, egg, all-bran, and milk into blender container. Cover; blend at high speed until well mixed. Pour over dry ingredients; stir just until moistened. Fill muffin cups two-thirds full. Bake 15 minutes or until done. *Makes 12 muffins.*

GOLDEN CORN BREAD

1 cup sifted all-purpose
   flour
1 cup yellow cornmeal
½ teaspoon salt
⅓ cup sugar

4 teaspoons baking powder
2 eggs
⅓ cup melted butter or
   margarine
1 cup milk

Heat oven to 425° F. Grease 8 x 8 x 2-inch baking pan. Combine flour, cornmeal, salt, sugar, and baking powder in medium-size bowl. Put remaining ingredients into blender container in order listed. Cover; blend at low speed until well mixed. Add dry ingredients to blender container in three additions. Cover; blend at low speed after each addition just until mixed. Pour into baking pan. Bake 25 to 30 minutes or until top is golden brown. *Makes one 8-inch square bread.*

Golden Corn Muffins: Fill twelve greased 2½-inch muffin-pan cups two-thirds full with batter. Bake 15 to 20 minutes or until golden brown.

BANANA BREAD

1¾ cups sifted all-purpose
   flour
2 teaspoons baking powder
¼ teaspoon baking soda
1 teaspoon salt
2 eggs

2 to 3 ripe bananas, cut up
   (2 cups)
⅓ cup softened butter or
   margarine
⅔ cup sugar

Heat oven to 350° F. Grease 9 x 5 x 3-inch loaf pan. Sift flour, baking powder, baking soda, and salt into medium-size bowl. Put eggs, bananas, butter, and sugar into blender container. Cover; blend at high speed until smooth. If necessary, stop blender during processing and push ingredients toward blades with rubber spatula. Pour over dry ingredients; stir just until moistened. Pour into prepared pan. Bake 40 to 45 minutes or until done. Cool in pan 10 minutes; remove from pan. Cool several hours before slicing. *Makes 1 loaf.*

Banana-Nut Bread: Add ⅔ cup walnuts to blended banana mixture in blender container. Cover; blend at medium speed just until nuts are chopped. Proceed as for Banana Bread.

Holiday Orange-Banana Bread: Put ¾ cup walnuts into blender container. Cover; ◾blend at medium speed until chopped. Add chopped nuts and 1 cup mixed candied fruit to bowl with dry ingredients. Put 1 small orange, peeled, seeded, and quartered, into blender container with remaining ingredients before blending. Proceed as for Banana Bread.

SOUR CREAM COFFEE CAKE

1½ cups sugar	¾ teaspoon baking soda
½ cup pecans	½ teaspoon salt
1 teaspoon ground cinnamon	½ cup softened butter or margarine
2 cups sifted all-purpose flour	½ teaspoon vanilla
1 teaspoon baking powder	2 eggs
	1 cup sour cream

Heat oven to 350° F. Grease 9 x 9 x 2-inch baking pan. Put ½ cup sugar, pecans, and cinnamon into blender container. Cover; ◾blend at medium speed until nuts are chopped. Empty onto wax paper; set aside. Sift flour, baking powder, baking soda, and salt into medium-size bowl; set aside. Put butter, 1 cup sugar, vanilla, and eggs into blender container. Cover; blend at high speed until well mixed. While blender is running, tip center cap and add half the flour mixture and ½ cup sour cream. If necessary, stop blender during processing and push ingredients toward blades with rubber spatula. Add remaining flour mixture and sour cream. Cover; blend at high speed until mixed. Pour half the batter into prepared pan. Sprinkle evenly with half the sugar-nut mixture. Repeat layers. Bake 40 to 45 minutes or until done. Cool 15 minutes. Cut into squares and serve warm. *Makes one 9-inch square cake.*

LEMON-NUT COFFEE CAKE

Batter:
  ½ cup walnuts
  2 cups packaged biscuit mix
  ½ cup milk
  1 egg
  ½ cup firmly packed brown
      sugar
  3 tablespoons melted butter
      or margarine
  ½ lemon rind
  1 tablespoon lemon juice

Topping:
  ½ cup walnuts
  1 cup cornflakes
  ¼ cup sugar
  ½ teaspoon ground
      cinnamon
  ½ cup melted butter or
      margarine

Have all ingredients at room temperature. Heat oven to 400° F. Grease 8 x 8 x 2-inch baking pan. *Prepare Topping:* Put walnuts into blender container. Cover; ⊓ blend at medium speed until chopped. Empty into small bowl. Put cornflakes into blender container. Cover; blend at medium speed until crumbed. Add to nuts; stir in sugar, cinnamon, and butter; mix well. *Prepare Batter:* Put walnuts into blender container. Cover; ⊓ blend at medium speed until chopped. Empty into medium-size bowl. Add biscuit mix. Put milk, egg, sugar, melted butter, lemon rind, and lemon juice into blender container. Cover; blend at medium speed until rind is chopped. Add to biscuit mix and nuts. Stir just until moistened. Pour into prepared pan. Sprinkle evenly with topping. Bake 25 minutes or until done. *Makes 1 cake.*

Down Home Breakfast
Fresh Tomato Juice (page 51)
Scrambled Eggs (page 112)
Crisp Bacon
Old-Fashioned Pancakes (page 132)
Coffee

WHITE BREAD

1 cup milk
2 tablespoons butter or
   margarine
2 tablespoons sugar
1 tablespoon salt
1 cup warm water (105° to
   115° F.)

2 packages active dry yeast
5 cups sifted all-purpose
   flour
Melted butter or
   margarine

Scald milk. Stir in butter, sugar, and salt; set aside to cool to lukewarm. Put warm water and yeast into blender container; let stand 3 to 5 minutes. Cover; blend at low speed until mixed. Add cooled milk mixture. Cover; blend at low speed until mixed. Add 1 cup flour. Cover; blend at high speed until smooth. Add 1 more cup flour. Cover; blend at high speed until smooth. If necessary, stop blender during processing and push ingredients toward blades with rubber spatula. Turn dough out onto heavily floured board. Knead in as much of remaining 3 cups flour as needed to make an elastic dough. Put dough into large, greased bowl; brush top with melted butter or margarine. Cover with double thickness of plastic wrap or clean towel; let rise in warm place (85° F.) about 1 hour or until double in bulk. Punch dough down; turn out onto floured board; knead 1 minute. Divide dough in half; shape each half into loaf. Put each loaf into greased 9 x 5 x 3-inch loaf pan. Cover; let rise 30 to 40 minutes or until almost double in bulk. Heat oven to 375° F. Bake 30 to 40 minutes or until bread is golden brown and sounds hollow when tapped on bottom. *Makes 2 loaves*.

EASY REFRIGERATOR ROLLS

1¾ cups warm water (105° to 115° F.)

2 packages active dry yeast

½ cup sugar

1 tablespoon salt

1 egg

¼ cup softened butter or margarine

6 cups sifted all-purpose flour

Melted butter or margarine

Put water and yeast into blender container; let stand 3 to 5 minutes. Cover; blend at low speed until mixed. Add sugar, salt, egg, and butter. Cover; blend at low speed until smooth. Add 3 cups flour. Cover; blend at high speed until smooth. If necessary, stop blender during processing and push ingredients toward blades with rubber spatula. Put remaining 3 cups flour into large mixing bowl. Add mixture from blender container; stir with wooden spoon to mix. Work dough with hands until smooth. Brush top of dough with melted butter. Cover with double thickness of plastic wrap or clean towel. Let rise in refrigerator at least 2 hours or until double in bulk. Punch dough down. Dough is now ready to shape into rolls. (It may be stored in refrigerator up to three days if it is punched down once each day.) When ready to bake, heat oven to 400° F. Shape rolls according to following directions and bake 12 to 15 minutes. Serve hot. *Makes 3 dozen rolls*.

Parker House Rolls: Roll dough out on lightly floured surface to ½-inch thickness. Cut into rounds with lightly floured 2½-inch biscuit cutter. Press deep crease, just off center, across each round with dull edge of knife. Brush rounds lightly with melted butter. Fold smaller section over larger; press edge lightly to seal with tines of a fork. Place, 1 inch apart, on lightly greased cookie sheet. Let rise in warm place (85° F.) about 20 minutes or until double in bulk. Brush with melted butter. *Makes 1 dozen rolls*.

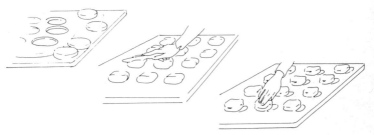

Cloverleaf Rolls: Divide dough in half. Roll each half with palms of hands on lightly floured surface into 18-inch-long rope. Cut each rope into eighteen equal pieces. Shape each piece into ball, tucking edges under so that top is smooth. Place three balls in each greased 2½-inch muffin-pan cup. Cover with clean towel. Let rise in warm place (85° F.) about 20 minutes or until double in bulk. Brush with melted butter or margarine. *Makes 1 dozen rolls*.

Pan Rolls: Roll dough with palms of hands on lightly floured surface into 12-inch-long strip. Cut into twelve equal pieces. Shape each piece into ball, tucking edges under so that top is smooth. Place ¼ inch apart in greased 8 or 9-inch round cake pan. Cover with clean towel. Let rise in warm place (85° F.) about 20 minutes or until double in bulk. Brush with melted butter or margarine. *Makes 1 dozen rolls*.

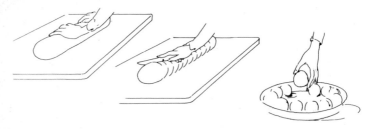

Easy Sweet Rolls: Follow directions for Easy Refrigerator Rolls, using two eggs instead of one and increasing softened butter to ½ cup. Use dough to make Prune or Apricot Swirls or Cheese Buns.

If you'd like to give your freshly baked loaf of bread a softer crust, brush the top of the loaf with melted butter or margarine after removing it from the pan.

PRUNE SWIRLS

1½ cups stewed pitted prunes, drained
¼ cup syrup from prunes
3 tablespoons sugar
1 tablespoon lemon juice
Thin strip lemon rind
¼ teaspoon ground cinnamon
½ recipe Easy Sweet Rolls dough (page 144)

Put prunes, syrup, sugar, lemon juice, rind, and cinnamon into blender container. Cover; blend at medium speed until smooth. Pour into saucepan; cook over low heat, stirring frequently, until mixture is thick enough to mound when dropped from spoon. Chill 30 minutes. Roll dough out on lightly floured surface to rectangle about ½ inch thick. Spread prune filling over dough to within 1 inch of edges. Roll up jelly-roll fashion, rolling tightly to seal in filling. Pinch edges firmly to seal seam. Cut into 1-inch-thick slices; place, cut sides down, 2 inches apart on lightly greased cookie sheets. Cover with clean towel. Let rise about 1 hour or until double in bulk. Heat oven to 400° F. Bake swirls 15 to 20 minutes or until golden brown. *Makes 2 dozen swirls.*

Apricot Swirls: Substitute 1½ cups drained, pitted canned apricots and ¼ cup syrup from apricots for prunes and prune syrup. Proceed as for Prune Swirls.

CHEESE BUNS

1 cup creamed cottage cheese	Thin strip lemon rind
⅓ cup sugar	½ recipe Easy Sweet Rolls dough (page 144)
1 egg yolk	Sugar
½ teaspoon vanilla	

Put cottage cheese, ⅓ cup sugar, egg yolk, vanilla, and lemon rind into blender container. Cover; blend at high speed until smooth. Chill 30 minutes. Roll dough out on lightly floured surface to ½-inch thickness. Cut into 2-inch squares. Place about 1 tablespoon cheese mixture in center of each square. Bring two opposite points to center; repeat with remaining two points; press gently to seal in filling. Place 2 inches apart on lightly greased cookie sheets. Cover with clean towel. Let rise in warm place (85° F.) 1 hour or until double in bulk. Sprinkle lightly with sugar. Heat oven to 400° F. Bake 15 minutes or until golden brown. *Makes 1½ dozen buns.*

Crêpes

All the recipes for both crêpe batters and fillings that follow incorporate the blender technique and are thus quick and easy to make. Mastering the technique of actually transforming the crêpe batter into crêpes may seem tedious at first, but after making the first two or three, the rest will be a snap. Of course, it's the fillings that provide the "pièce de résistance." And once you've prepared that, then you can decide which of many ways to put together the dish. Crêpes may be filled, rolled, and served in a single layer; rolled and stacked in a casserole with a special sauce; or filled flat, stacked like a torte, topped—perhaps even "nutted" for a change of pace—and cut into wedges to serve.

Secrets to Crêpe Cookery

Crêpe batter should be the consistency of light cream, just thick enough to coat a wooden spoon. If batter is too thick, thin it by beating in a little water, adding very small amounts at a time. If too thin, mix 1 or 2 tablespoons of flour into the batter.

147

A cooked crêpe should be about $1/16$ of an inch thick, smooth, and lightly browned.

Prepare your first crêpe or two as a test for consistency of the batter, the proper amount of heat, and the right amount of batter. Discard test crêpes until you achieve the desired result. (Usually the first two or three will have a lacy pattern, which is not the desired look.)

If your crêpe has too many bubbles, either mix the batter at a lower speed or let the batter stand at least 1 hour before baking. If small holes form in the center of a crêpe as it cooks, drop small amounts of batter over the holes with a spoon or spatula. If the batter sticks to the pan, check the directions for oiling and seasoning.

If the edges of the crêpe are too crisp and brittle, the batter is probably too thin or the pan too hot. Try thickening the batter or decreasing the heat.

Opposite: Crêpes Florentine, page 150.

CREPES

1 cup milk
2 eggs
1 cup all-purpose flour

¼ teaspoon salt
2 tablespoons melted butter
or margarine

Put all ingredients into blender container in order listed. Cover; blend at high speed 1 minute. Let batter stand at room temperature 1 hour. Bake in hot, greased 6 to 7-inch skillet, using 2 tablespoons batter for each crêpe, or in 8 to 8½-inch skillet, using 3 tablespoons batter. Tilt pan to make a very thin crêpe. When crêpe is delicately brown on underside, turn to brown second side. Remove crêpe. Repeat with remaining batter. As crêpes are cooked, stack with wax paper between until ready to use. *Makes 16 to 20 six-inch crêpes or 12 eight-inch crêpes.*

Note: If using upside-down crêpe griddle, follow manufacturer's recipe and directions for baking crêpes.

Whole Wheat Crêpes: Use whole wheat flour in place of all-purpose flour and increase milk to 1⅓ cups. Proceed as for Crêpes.

Dessert Crêpes: Add 2 tablespoons sugar to blender container with other ingredients. Proceed as for Crêpes.

SEAFOOD CREPES

1 recipe Crêpes (page 148)
1½ cups Sauce Mornay (page 172)

2 cans (6 ounces each) crabmeat or tuna, drained and flaked, or 3 cans (4½ ounces each) small shrimp, drained

Prepare Crêpes in 6-inch skillet; set aside. Heat oven to 400° F. Add ¾ cup Mornay Sauce to seafood; mix well. Spoon about 2 tablespoons seafood mixture in center of each crêpe; roll up. Place filled crêpes in single layer in greased, shallow baking dish. Spoon remaining ¾ cup Mornay Sauce over crêpes. Bake about 20 minutes or until crêpes are thoroughly heated and top is golden brown. *Makes 6 to 8 servings.*

CHICKEN CREPES

1 recipe Crêpes or Whole Wheat Crêpes (page 148)
2 cups Chicken Velouté Sauce (page 171)

1½ cups cubed cooked chicken
¼ cup heavy cream

Prepare Crêpes in 6-inch skillet; set aside. Heat oven to 400° F. Prepare thick Chicken Velouté Sauce using 6 tablespoons butter and 6 tablespoons flour. Add 1 cup sauce to chicken; mix well. Spoon 2 tablespoons chicken mixture in center of each crêpe; roll up. Place filled crêpes in single layer in greased, shallow baking dish. Whip cream; fold into remaining 1 cup Chicken Velouté Sauce. Spoon over crêpes. Bake about 20 minutes or until crêpes are heated through and top is golden brown. *Makes 6 to 8 servings.*

CHEESE BLINTZES

1 recipe Dessert Crêpes (page 148)
2½ cups creamed cottage cheese
2 egg yolks

1 tablespoon sugar
1½ teaspoons vanilla or lemon juice
2 tablespoons butter or margarine

Prepare Dessert Crêpes in 8-inch skillet. Put cottage cheese, egg yolks, sugar, and vanilla into blender container. Cover; blend at high speed until smooth. Spoon about 2 tablespoons cheese mixture on each crêpe. Fold crêpes over from opposite sides, then into envelope shape. Heat butter in large skillet. Cook blintzes, a few at a time, until brown on both sides. *Makes 6 servings*.

Serving Suggestion: Serve with sugar and cinnamon, preserves, or sour cream.

CREPES FLORENTINE

1 recipe Crêpes or Whole
    Wheat Crêpes (page 148)
¼ cup cubed Parmesan
    cheese
2 packages (10 ounces each)
    frozen chopped spinach,
    thawed and well drained

1½ cups Sauce Mornay (page
    172)
Dash nutmeg

Prepare Crêpes in 6-inch skillet; set aside. Heat oven to 400° F. Start blender at medium speed. While blender is running, tip center cap and gradually add Parmesan cheese, blending until grated. Empty onto wax paper; set aside. Prepare Mornay Sauce; add nutmeg. Measure ¾ cup Mornay sauce and set aside. Stir spinach into remaining sauce. Spoon about 2 tablespoons spinach mixture in center of cooked crêpe; roll up. Place filled crêpes in single layer in greased, shallow baking dish. Stir grated Parmesan cheese into reserved Mornay Sauce. Spoon over crêpes. Bake about 15 minutes or until sauce is bubbly and top is golden brown. *Makes 6 to 8 servings*.

CREPES SUZETTE

1 recipe Dessert Crêpes (page 148)	½ cup softened butter or margarine
1 large orange	¼ cup orange-flavored liqueur
2 thin strips lemon rind	Brandy
½ cup sugar	

Prepare Dessert Crêpes in 6-inch skillet; set aside. Remove rind from orange with vegetable peeler; set rind aside. Squeeze orange (you should have ½ cup juice). Put orange juice and orange and lemon rinds into blender container. Cover; blend at medium speed until rinds are finely chopped. Add sugar, butter, and orange-flavored liqueur. Cover; blend at high speed until smooth. Pour into large skillet or chafing dish. Heat one crêpe at a time in sauce, turning quickly with spoon and fork; fold crêpe in quarters. Move folded crêpes to side of pan, arranging them in overlapping circle. Spoon brandy over crêpes. Ignite with long match. Slide pan back and forth gently, spooning flaming liquid over crêpes until flames die down. *Makes 6 to 8 servings.*

CREPES DE CACAO

1 recipe Dessert Crêpes (page 148)	¾ cup softened butter or margarine
8 to 10 macaroons	1 cup heavy cream
⅓ cup crème de cacao	Crème de cacao
⅓ cup sugar	

Prepare Dessert Crêpes in 6-inch skillet; set aside. Break four macaroons into blender container. Cover; blend at medium speed until finely crumbed. Empty into measuring cup. Repeat process with remaining macaroons (you should have ½ cup crumbs). Put ⅓ cup crème de cacao, sugar, and ½ cup butter into blender container. Cover; blend at high speed until smooth. Empty into mixing bowl; stir in macaroon crumbs. Spread mixture evenly over crêpes; roll up. Whip cream. To serve, heat remaining ¼ cup butter in large skillet or chafing dish. Add crêpes; heat thoroughly. Top each serving with whipped cream and a drizzle of crème de cacao. *Makes 6 to 8 servings.*

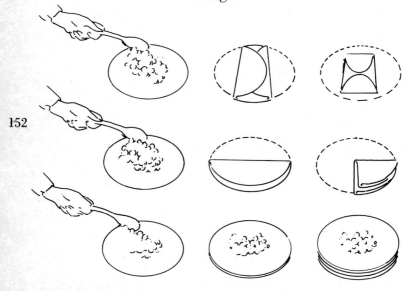

Folding Crêpes

While fillings and batter create variety, the way a crêpe is folded creates eye appeal. Consider the traditional Hungarian custom, for example, of serving three crêpes at a time, each one folded differently and each containing a different filling. Here are some traditional folds:

Rolled Crêpe: Spread the filling on the crêpe and roll

up from one side.

Envelope Crêpe: Place the filling in the center and fold two sides over the center.

Pocket Crêpe: Fold as for the Envelope Crêpe and then tuck the two open ends into the crêpe.

Triangle Crêpe: Place the filling in the center, fold in half, and then in half again to form a triangle. This is the traditional fold for Crêpes Suzette.

Stacked Crêpes: Place filling on one crêpe, top with a second, fill, and proceed in this way until you reach the desired height. Cut in wedges to serve.

Elegant Brunch
Fresh Peach Nectar (Page 52)
Crêpes Florentine (page 150)
Sausage Links
Buttered English Muffins
Coffee

HUNGARIAN NUT CREPE STACK

1 recipe Dessert Crêpes
   (page 148)
½ cup walnuts

1 recipe Sweetened
   Whipped Cream (page
   207)
Hot Fudge Sauce (page 207)

Prepare Dessert Crêpes in 8-inch skillet; set aside. Put walnuts into blender container. Cover; blend at medium speed until ground. Fold nuts into Sweetened Whipped Cream. Spread one crêpe evenly with about 1½ tablespoons cream mixture. Top with second crêpe; spread with cream. Continue until six crêpes have been spread and stacked. Repeat with remaining six crêpes and whipped cream mixture to make second stack. Chill stacks. Cut in wedges and serve topped with Hot Fudge Sauce. *Makes 8 servings.*

Salads

A salad is an area where you can allow your own creativity full rein. Whether it is to be a crisp, fresh accompaniment to the meal or the main dish for a luncheon or supper, a salad recipe should be considered only a basic guide, to be supplemented by your imagination. Add a vegetable here, substitute a fruit there. Use fresh, frozen, and canned products, sometimes in halves or slices, sometimes blender-chopped. Experiment with different types of dressings and seasonings.

Secrets to Preparing Greens for Salads

Wash and store greens properly—as soon as they are brought home, wash, dry, and refrigerate them according to the following procedures:

Remove and discard any outer leaves of a head of lettuce that are bruised. Cut out the core with a sharp knife or rap it sharply with the heel of your hand and pull it out; hold the head under cold running water so that it fills the cavity that once held the core. With greens such as escarole, chicory, and romaine, leave the root ends but wash the leaves thoroughly under cold running water.

Shake excess water off greens and blot each leaf.

Store washed green leaves in a crisper in the refrigerator. If you plan to keep them for any length of time, place them in transparent plastic wrap, plastic bags, or a special airtight plastic container. Store watercress and parsley in tightly covered jars or sealed plastic bags after washing and drying them.

Instead of cutting them, tear greens into bite-size pieces when preparing salad bowls—they will be more attractive and less likely to wilt or discolor.

Mix several greens in salads to achieve contrasts in texture and color.

Avoid the use of too much dressing—it will cause a salad to wilt. A general rule of thumb is to use ¼ cup of dressing to each 1½ quarts of greens.

Add dressing just before serving unless marinating.

Opposite: Calico Slaw, page 157; Sour Cream Dressing, page 167.

Secrets to Making Molded Salads

Layer a salad by chilling the first portion just until set—that is, until the first layer is set but the surface is still slightly tacky. That stickiness is necessary to enable the second layer to stick to the first.

If you wish to create a design for the top of a molded salad, spoon enough of the liquid gelatin into the bottom of the mold to form a thin layer. Chill until set, either by placing it in the refrigerator or by setting it into a bed of cracked or crushed ice (see page 20). Then arrange a design made up of cut vegetables, fruit, meat, etc., on the just-set gelatin; spoon another thin layer of gelatin over it and chill it again until it is firm. Continue by following recipe directions.

Chill all finished gelatin salads until set. Allow several hours or overnight for this step.

Unmold a gelatin salad by selecting a plate that is large enough to hold the salad and its garnish. Rinse the plate in cold water so that you will be able to move the salad in case it is not centered properly after unmolding. Run the tip of a small, sharp knife carefully around the edge of the gelatin to loosen it from the sides of the mold. Dip the mold into warm, not hot, water until the water comes to the level of the top surface of the gelatin; *leave it in the water only a few seconds*. Place the plate over the mold and invert it, holding the plate and the mold together. Shake them gently until the gelatin has been released. Lift off the mold. If the gelatin does not come out of the mold the first time, redip it quickly in warm water or tip the mold slightly to the side.

156

CABBAGE SLAW

1 medium head green cabbage, cored and coarsely cut up	1 cup Sour Cream Dressing (page 167)

Put cabbage into blender container to 5-cup mark; add water just to cover. Cover; ◼blend at medium speed just until chopped. Drain thoroughly in colander; empty into large bowl. Repeat process with remaining cabbage. Toss with Sour Cream Dressing. *Makes 6 servings*.

Red Cabbage Slaw: Substitute 1 medium head red cabbage for green cabbage, or use half red cabbage and half green cabbage. Proceed as for Cabbage Slaw.

Calico Slaw: Substitute ½ red cabbage and ½ green cabbage for medium head green cabbage. Add 2 carrots, cut up, and ½ small onion, cut up. Proceed as for Cabbage Slaw.

CARROT-RAISIN SALAD

4 large carrots, pared and
   cut up
½ cup seedless raisins
½ teaspoon salt

Dash pepper
½ to ¾ cup Sour Cream
   Dressing (page 167)

Put carrots into blender container. Add cold water to cover. Cover; ■ blend at medium speed just until carrots are chopped. Drain thoroughly in colander. Empty into bowl. Add raisins, salt, and pepper. Toss with Sour Cream Dressing. *Makes 4 servings*.

MOLDED CHICKEN SALAD

2 tablespoons dry sherry
1 teaspoon lemon juice
1 envelope unflavored
   gelatin
½ cup boiling chicken broth,
   or ½ chicken bouillon
   cube dissolved in ½ cup
   boiling water
¼ cup mayonnaise
¼ teaspoon dry mustard
   Few dashes hot pepper
   sauce

2 sprigs parsley
1 thin slice onion
½ green pepper, seeded and
   cut up
3 stalks celery, cut up
1 canned pimiento, cut up
2 cups cubed cooked
   chicken
   Salad greens

Put sherry and lemon juice into blender container.

Sprinkle on gelatin; let stand 1 minute. Add boiling broth. Cover; blend at low speed until gelatin is dissolved. Add remaining ingredients except chicken and salad greens in order listed. Cover; blend at medium speed just until vegetables are coarsely chopped. Add chicken. Cover; blend at medium speed just until all chicken goes through blades. If necessary, stop blender during processing and push ingredients toward blades with rubber spatula. Pour into 1½-quart mold or 9 x 5 x 3-inch loaf pan. Chill several hours or until firm. Unmold onto salad greens. *Makes 6 servings.*

Molded Tuna Salad: Omit sherry, increase lemon juice to 2 tablespoons, and substitute two cans (6½ or 7 ounces each) tuna, drained and flaked, for chicken. Proceed as for Molded Chicken Salad. Garnish with lemon slices.

SALMON MOUSSE

3 tablespoons lemon juice
2 tablespoons cold water
2 envelopes unflavored
  gelatin
⅔ cup boiling water
2 stalks celery, cut up
¼ medium cucumber, pared
  and cut up
1 thin slice onion
½ cup mayonnaise

1 cup heavy cream
1 can (16 ounces) salmon,
  drained, boned, and
  flaked
¾ teaspoon salt
Dash cayenne pepper
Salad greens
Ripe olives and pimiento
  (optional)

Put lemon juice and cold water into blender container. Sprinkle on gelatin; let stand 1 minute. Add boiling water. Cover; blend at low speed until gelatin is dissolved. Add remaining ingredients except salad greens, olives, and pimiento to blender container in order listed. Cover; blend at high speed until mixture is smooth. Pour into 5-cup fish or other mold. Chill several hours or until firm. Unmold on salad greens. Garnish with olive slices and pimiento strips if desired. *Makes 6 servings*.

MOLDED CRABMEAT SALAD

⅓ cup vinegar
2 envelopes unflavored gelatin
½ cup boiling water
2 cups sour cream
2 teaspoons salt
2 cans (6 ounces each) crabmeat, drained and boned

2 small cucumbers, pared and cut up
2 thin slices onion
Salad greens
Cucumber and radish slices (optional)

Put vinegar into blender container. Sprinkle on gelatin; let stand 1 minute. Add boiling water. Cover; blend at low speed until gelatin is dissolved. Add sour cream and salt. Cover; blend at medium speed until smooth. Add crabmeat, cucumber, and onion. Cover; blend at medium speed just until vegetables are chopped. Pour into 1½-quart mold. Chill several hours or until firm. Unmold onto salad greens. Garnish with cucumber and radish slices if desired. *Makes 6 to 8 servings*.

159

AVOCADO MOLD

¼ cup lemon juice
2 envelopes unflavored gelatin
1 cup boiling water
3 ripe avocados, peeled, pitted, and cut up

1 cup sour cream
½ small onion, cut up
1 teaspoon salt
⅛ teaspoon pepper
Salad greens

Put lemon juice into blender container. Sprinkle on gelatin; let stand 1 minute. Add boiling water. Cover; blend at low speed until gelatin is dissolved. Add remaining ingredients except salad greens to blender container in order listed. Cover; blend at high speed until smooth. Pour into 6-cup ring or other mold. Press plastic wrap against surface. Chill several hours or until firm. Unmold onto salad greens just before serving. *Makes 6 to 8 servings.*

Serving Suggestion: If using a ring mold, fill the center with a seafood salad.

PERFECTION SALAD

1 package (4-serving size) lemon flavor gelatin
1 cup boiling water
¾ cup pineapple juice
1 medium carrot, pared and cut up

1 cup coarsely cut cabbage
1 tablespoon lemon juice
½ teaspoon salt
Salad greens

Put gelatin and boiling water into blender container. Cover; blend at low speed until gelatin is dissolved. Add remaining ingredients except salad greens to blender container in order listed. Cover; blend at medium speed just until vegetables are chopped. Chill until slightly thickened. Stir gently to disperse vegetables. Pour into 3-cup mold or into individual molds. Chill until firm. Unmold onto salad greens. *Makes 4 to 6 servings.*

BEET AND CUCUMBER RELISH SALAD

1 package (4-serving size) lime or lemon flavor gelatin
¾ teaspoon salt
1 can (16 ounces) sliced or diced beets
1 thin slice onion
1 tablespoon vinegar

1 teaspoon prepared horseradish
⅔ cup cracked or crushed ice
½ medium cucumber, pared and cut up
Salad greens

Put gelatin and salt into blender container. Drain liquid from beets; measure ¾ cup liquid; heat to boiling. Pour into blender container. Cover; blend at low speed until gelatin is dissolved. Add onion, vinegar, horseradish, and ice. Cover; blend at medium speed until ice is melted. Add cucumber and drained beets. Cover; blend at medium speed just until vegetables are coarsely chopped. Pour into 1-quart ring mold or into individual molds. Chill until slightly thickened. Stir gently to disperse vegetables. Chill until firm. Unmold on salad greens. *Makes 4 to 6 servings.*

TOMATO-CHEESE ASPIC

1 can (18 ounces) tomato juice
2 envelopes unflavored gelatin
1 teaspoon sugar
½ teaspoon salt
2 stalks celery, cut up
1 thin slice onion

2 packages (3 ounces each) cream cheese, cubed and softened
¼ cup stuffed green olives
1 cup cracked or crushed ice
Salad greens

Put ½ cup tomato juice into blender container. Sprinkle on gelatin. Add sugar and salt. Heat remaining tomato juice to boiling in small saucepan. Pour into blender container. Cover; blend at low speed until gelatin is dissolved. Add celery, onion, and cream cheese. Cover; blend at medium speed until vegetables are chopped. Add olives and ice. Cover; blend at medium speed until ice is melted. Pour into 5-cup mold. Chill several hours or until firm. Unmold onto salad greens. *Makes 6 to 8 servings.*

Salad Dressings

It is the salad dressing that adds character to a salad. In choosing a dressing, remember that it should complement the ingredients and the flavor, not overpower them. Try different types of dressings. Experiment with different oils and vinegars. Substitute lemon juice or lime juice for the vinegar, or mix them together. Change the herb from oregano to thyme or marjoram; switch from basil to tarragon, or add a touch of nutmeg or allspice.

Whatever ingredients you choose to combine in your dressing, keep in mind that the blender will make quick work of mixing them; it will also help to hold the flavors and the body together. Make enough to store in special blend-in, store-in containers in the refrigerator for later use.

MAYONNAISE

1 egg	2 tablespoons lemon juice
1 egg yolk	1 tablespoon vinegar
¾ teaspoon salt	1½ cups vegetable oil
¾ teaspoon dry mustard	

Put egg, egg yolk, salt, mustard, lemon juice, vinegar, and ½ cup oil into blender container. Cover; blend at high speed until mixed. While blender is running, tip center cap and add remaining 1 cup oil in a slow, steady stream. *Makes 2 cups.*

Mayonnaise Chaud-Froid: Sprinkle one envelope unflavored gelatin over ¼ cup cold water in small bowl. Let stand 5 minutes. Set bowl over boiling water; stir until gelatin is dissolved. Put gelatin mixture and 1 cup mayonnaise into blender container. Cover; blend at high speed until smooth. Use to coat eggs, ham, chicken, fish, etc.

Note: If mayonnaise separates or is too thin, the ingredients may not have been at room temperature or the oil may have been added too rapidly, causing the emulsion to break. However, you can easily salvage the ingredients. Pour the broken emulsion into a pitcher or other container. Wash and dry blender container. Break one egg into container; cover and run on low speed. While blender is running, slowly add the broken emulsion. When mixture reaches top of blender blades, run on high speed, continuing to add the separated mayonnaise slowly.

Dinner for Two
Clam-Tomato Consommé (page 228)
Chicken Breasts Supreme (page 95)
Pilaf (page 116)
Broccoli Polonaise (page 120)
Curly Endive   Parmesan Dressing (page 166)
Pears Hélène (page 187)
Cappuccino (page 50)

Celebration Dinner
Chicken Liver Pâté (page 37)
Standing Rib Roast
Cauliflower au Gratin (page 121)
Avocado Mold (page 159)   Mayonnaise (page 162)
Dry Red Wine
Crêpes Suzette (page 151)
Demitasse

RUSSIAN DRESSING

1 cup mayonnaise
¼ cup chili sauce or catsup
1 thin slice onion
1 teaspoon prepared
  horseradish

1 teaspoon lemon juice
½ teaspoon Worcestershire
  sauce

Put all ingredients into blender container in order listed. Cover; blend at high speed until well combined. *Makes 1⅓ cups.*

THOUSAND ISLAND DRESSING

3 sprigs parsley
¼ cup stuffed green olives
1 hard-cooked egg, shelled
1 thin slice onion
¼ cup chili sauce

1 teaspoon prepared
  horseradish
1 teaspoon lemon juice
1 cup mayonnaise

Start blender on high speed. While blender is
running, tip center cap and gradually add parsley,
olives, and egg, blending until chopped. Add
remaining ingredients to blender container in order
listed. Cover; blend at low speed until mixed.
Makes 1½ cups.

Last-Minute Get Together—Make It Italian
Anchovies   Roasted Peppers
Spaghetti with Meat Sauce (page 177)
Green Salad   Italian Dressing (page 166)
Italian Bread
Biscuit Tortoni (page 192)

164

GREEN GODDESS DRESSING

1 green onion with top, cut
  up
1 clove garlic, halved
¼ cup parsley sprigs
3 anchovies
1 tablespoon lemon juice

1 tablespoon tarragon
  vinegar
½ teaspoon salt
¼ teaspoon pepper
1 cup mayonnaise
½ cup sour cream

Start blender at high speed. While blender is
running, tip center cap and add onion, then garlic,
then parsley, then anchovies to blender container,
blending until chopped. Add remaining ingredients
to blender container in order listed. Cover; blend at
low speed until mixed. *Makes 1⅔ cups.*

Serving Suggestions: Serve with cold salmon and other fish or with green salads.

CREAMY ROQUEFORT OR BLUE CHEESE DRESSING

1 cup mayonnaise
1 tablespoon white wine
   vinegar
½ teaspoon Worcestershire
   sauce

¼ teaspoon salt
⅛ teaspoon pepper
Dash hot pepper sauce
3 ounces Roquefort or blue
   cheese, crumbled

Put all ingredients into blender container in order listed. Cover; blend at low speed until combined. *Makes 1⅓ cups.*

FRENCH DRESSING

¾ cup olive or vegetable oil
¼ cup wine or cider vinegar
   or lemon juice
1 teaspoon salt

¼ teaspoon dry mustard
¼ teaspoon sugar
⅛ teaspoon pepper
Dash paprika

Put all ingredients into blender container in order listed. Cover; blend at high speed until combined. *Makes 1 cup.*

Creamy French Dressing: Add ¼ cup mayonnaise. Proceed as for French Dressing.

Blue Cheese French Dressing: Add 4 ounces blue cheese, crumbled. Proceed as for French Dressing.

Chiffonade Dressing: Add ⅓ cup sliced or diced cooked beets, five sprigs parsley, and one cut-up green onion, white part only. Proceed as for French Dressing. Add two shelled hard-cooked eggs. Cover; blend at low speed just until chopped.

HONEY FRENCH DRESSING 🧂

¾ cup vegetable oil
¼ cup lemon juice
½ cup honey
½ teaspoon Worcestershire
    sauce
¾ teaspoon salt

¼ teaspoon pepper
¼ teaspoon paprika
¼ teaspoon dry mustard
½ teaspoon celery or poppy
    seeds
Small piece lemon rind

Put all ingredients into blender container in order listed. Cover; blend at high speed until smooth. *Makes 1½ cups.*

ITALIAN DRESSING

3 cloves garlic, halved
¾ cup vegetable or olive oil
⅓ cup white vinegar

1 teaspoon salt
⅛ teaspoon pepper
¼ canned pimiento

Put garlic, oil, vinegar, salt, and pepper into blender container. Cover; blend at high speed until smooth. Add pimiento. Cover; blend at medium speed just until pimiento is chopped. *Makes 1 cup.*

PARMESAN DRESSING

¼ cup grated Parmesan
    cheese
2 eggs
1½ cups vegetable or olive oil
½ cup dry white wine
⅓ cup vinegar

1½ teaspoons seasoned salt
½ teaspoon pepper
½ teaspoon paprika
½ clove garlic
1 thin slice onion

Put all ingredients except onion into blender container in order listed. Cover; blend at high speed until smooth. Add onion. Cover; blend at medium speed just until chopped. *Makes 3 cups*.

Caesar Salad Dressing: Prepare Parmesan Dressing. Add two anchovies to blender container with onion. To serve, toss required amount of dressing with romaine in salad bowl; top with croutons.

BUTTERMILK BLUE CHEESE DRESSING 🧂

1 cup buttermilk	¼ teaspoon garlic powder
2 cups mayonnaise	½ pound blue cheese,
½ small onion, cut up	crumbled
1 tablespoon Worcestershire sauce	

Put buttermilk, mayonnaise, onion, Worcestershire, garlic powder, and half the cheese into blender container. Cover; blend at high speed until smooth. Add remaining cheese. Cover; blend at low speed until mixed. If a smooth dressing is preferred, blend until smooth. *Makes 4 cups*.

167

SOUR CREAM DRESSING 🧂

1¼ cups mayonnaise	2 tablespoons lemon juice
1 cup sour cream	Dash hot pepper sauce

Put all ingredients into blender container in order listed. Cover; blend at high speed until smooth. *Makes 2½ cups*.

Dill Sour Cream Dressing: Add ⅛ teaspoon dry mustard and four sprigs fresh dill or ½ teaspoon dried dill weed. Proceed as for Sour Cream Dressing.

Sauces

The blender can make the job of creating any sauce elementary, regardless of your cooking expertise. Suddenly, sauces become very simple, easy to make. And not only will they equal any made by a trained saucier in a fine restaurant, but their preparation time will be dramatically reduced. You will even be able to turn out— quickly—exquisite chef's sauces normally restricted to restaurant menus—Béarnaise, Mornay, or Rémoulade. A simple analysis of the recipes here will soon reveal the secret—your own blender-made mayonnaise or Hollandaise sauce combined with a little creativity. Add one of these to a boiled or broiled meat (even a hamburger), chicken, fish, maybe an omelet or a vegetable, and you'll have transformed a routine dinner into a banquet!

The blender can also help in the preparation of marinades, the thin sauces generally made with a vinegar, wine, or lemon juice base, seasoned with condiments and herbs, and used to flavor or tenderize food before it is cooked. Since inexpensive cuts of meat can be tenderized by marinating them, having a good repertory of marinades can be a way to stretch the budget. Leftover cooked vegetables can also be marinated and chilled to provide tangy side dishes appropriate to nearly any meal. Marinades are flavor-stretchers, too—for instance, many foods, such as shrimp or steaks, are marinated before being cooked over charcoal, which adds a strong flavor of its own.

Secrets to Sauce Cookery

If you want to create a truly fine sauce, use only the best ingredients.

Correct seasonings as you proceed with the recipe.

To capture the rich brown essence important to preparing many of the flavorful sauces and gravies, deglaze the pan in which meat or poultry has been roasted. To deglaze, discard all fat; add a small amount of stock, wine, or water to the roasting pan; stir, scraping up all bits and pieces, over low heat until all the flavor has been captured.

Another procedure in making rich and flavorful

Opposite: Pesto Sauce, page 179.

sauces is the reduction of a stock or broth to concentrate its flavor. To reduce, cook the liquid until it is less in volume by the amount specified in the recipe.

The traditional French method for making a white or brown sauce begins with preparing a roux, which is made by combining butter and flour and cooking them for several minutes *before the liquid is added*. This cooking helps eliminate the raw taste of flour and allows the flour particles to absorb the liquid smoothly. The blender method of combining the butter, flour, and liquid all at one time and then cooking achieves the same result, reduces preparation time, and always assures a smooth sauce.

Lumpy gravy can be made smooth by blending it at high speed until smooth.

A cream sauce will never lump if the butter, flour, and milk are blended before cooking.

Secrets to Making and Using Marinades

To tenderize meat with the marinade method, allow a minimum of 1 hour at room temperature, although 2 to 3 hours is better; if you wish to marinate a food the day before serving, refrigerate it and then remove it 1 hour before cooking to bring it to room temperature. Turn food several times during the marinating process so that the flavors will penetrate.

MEDIUM WHITE SAUCE

1 cup milk	¼ teaspoon salt
2 tablespoons softened butter or margarine	Dash pepper
2 tablespoons all-purpose flour	

Put all ingredients into blender container in order listed. Cover; blend at high speed until smooth. Pour into small saucepan. Cook over medium heat, stirring constantly, until mixture thickens and comes to a boil. *Makes about 1 cup*.

Thin White Sauce: Prepare Medium White Sauce using 1 tablespoon butter and 1 tablespoon flour.

Thick White Sauce: Prepare Medium White Sauce using 3 tablespoons butter and 3 tablespoons flour.

SAUCE BECHAMEL

1 cup milk	1 thin slice onion
2 tablespoons softened butter or margarine	¼ teaspoon salt Dash pepper
2 tablespoons all-purpose flour	Dash ground nutmeg ¼ cup light cream

Put all ingredients except cream into blender container in order listed. Cover; blend at medium speed until onion is finely chopped. Pour into small saucepan. Cook over medium heat, stirring constantly, until mixture thickens and comes to a boil. Reduce heat to very low; simmer about 5 minutes. Stir in cream and heat gently. *Makes about 1¼ cups*.

CHICKEN VELOUTE SAUCE

1 cup chicken broth, or 1 chicken bouillon cube dissolved in 1 cup hot water	2 tablespoons all-purpose flour
2 tablespoons softened butter or margarine	¼ teaspoon salt Dash pepper Dash ground nutmeg

Put all ingredients into blender container in order listed. Cover; blend at medium speed until smooth. Pour into small saucepan. Cook over medium heat, stirring constantly, until mixture thickens and comes to a boil. *Makes about 1 cup*.

SAUCE SUPREME

1 cup chicken broth, or 1 chicken bouillon cube dissolved in 1 cup hot water

2 tablespoons softened butter or margarine

2 tablespoons all-purpose flour

¼ teaspoon salt

Dash pepper

Dash ground nutmeg

¼ cup heavy cream

Put all ingredients except cream into blender container. Cover; blend at medium speed until smooth. Pour into small saucepan. Cook over medium heat, stirring constantly, until mixture thickens and comes to a boil. Stir in cream and heat gently. *Makes about 1½ cups.*

172

SAUCE MORNAY

1 cup milk

¼ cup cubed Gruyère cheese

3 tablespoons softened butter or margarine

3 tablespoons all-purpose flour

¼ teaspoon salt

Dash pepper

2 tablespoons grated Parmesan cheese

¼ cup light cream

Put milk, Gruyère cheese, butter, flour, salt, and pepper into blender container. Cover; blend at medium speed until smooth. Pour into small saucepan. Cook over medium heat, stirring constantly, until mixture thickens and comes to a boil. Stir in Parmesan cheese and cream; heat gently. *Makes about 1½ cups.*

A LA KING SAUCE

½ cup milk
½ cup light cream
3 tablespoons softened
  butter or margarine
3 tablespoons flour
¼ teaspoon salt

Dash pepper
¼ small green pepper,
  seeded and cut up
1 canned pimiento, cut up
3 parsley sprigs
2 tablespoons dry sherry

Put milk, cream, butter, flour, salt, and pepper into blender container. Cover; blend at medium speed until smooth. Add green pepper, pimiento, and parsley. Cover; blend at medium speed until chopped. Pour into small saucepan. Cook over medium heat, stirring constantly, until mixture thickens and comes to a boil. Stir in sherry and heat gently. *Makes 1½ cups*.

Serving Suggestion: Serve with diced cooked chicken, turkey, or tuna over rice or toast.

173

NEWBURG SAUCE

1 cup milk
3 tablespoons softened
  butter or margarine
3 tablespoons all-purpose
  flour

1 egg yolk
¼ teaspoon salt
Dash pepper
¼ cup heavy cream
2 tablespoons dry sherry

Put milk, butter, flour, egg yolk, salt, and pepper into blender container. Cover; blend at medium speed until smooth. Pour into small saucepan. Cook over medium heat, stirring constantly, until mixture thickens and comes to a boil. Stir in cream and sherry; heat gently. *Makes 1½ cups*.

Serving Suggestion: Serve with lobster, shrimp, or tuna over rice or toast.

CHEESE SAUCE

1 cup milk
3 tablespoons softened
    butter or margarine
3 tablespoons all-purpose
    flour

½ cup cubed sharp Cheddar
    cheese
¼ teaspoon dry mustard
¼ teaspoon salt
Dash pepper

Put all ingredients into blender container in order listed. Cover; blend at medium speed until smooth. Pour into small saucepan. Cook over medium heat, stirring constantly, until mixture thickens and comes to a boil. *Makes about 1½ cups.*

SAUCE NORMANDE

2 tablespoons softened
    butter or margarine
1 tablespoon all-purpose
    flour
1 bottle (8 ounces) clam
    juice

2 egg yolks
½ cup heavy cream
¼ teaspoon salt
⅛ teaspoon pepper

174

Put all ingredients into blender container in order listed. Cover; blend at medium speed until smooth. Pour into small saucepan. Cook over medium heat, stirring constantly, until mixture thickens and comes to a boil. *Makes about 1½ cups.*

HOLLANDAISE SAUCE

½ cup butter or margarine
3 egg yolks
3 tablespoons lemon juice

¼ teaspoon salt
Dash cayenne pepper

Heat butter in small saucepan until bubbling but not brown. Put remaining ingredients into blender container in order listed. Cover; blend at medium speed until thoroughly mixed. While blender is running, tip center cap and add hot butter in a slow, steady stream. Serve immediately or keep warm in top of double boiler over hot water. *Makes about ¾ cup.*

Serving Suggestion: Serve over cooked asparagus, broccoli, or other vegetables, poached salmon, or eggs Benedict.

Sauce Mousseline: Prepare Hollandaise Sauce as above. Beat ½ cup heavy cream until stiff; fold into Hollandaise. Serve with vegetables or fish. *Makes 1¼ cups.*

BEARNAISE SAUCE

2 tablespoons dry white wine
2 tablespoons tarragon vinegar
2 teaspoons dried chervil
1 teaspoon dried tarragon
2 thin slices onion
4 parsley sprigs
¼ teaspoon pepper
¾ cup Hollandaise Sauce (page 174)

Combine wine, vinegar, chervil, tarragon, onion, parsley, and pepper in small saucepan. Bring to a boil; boil rapidly 3 minutes or until reduced to about half its original volume. Prepare Hollandaise Sauce in blender. While blender is running, tip center cap and slowly add hot wine mixture. Blend at high speed until thoroughly mixed. *Makes 1 cup.*

Serving Suggestion: Serve with broiled meat or fish.

ALMOND BUTTER SAUCE

½ cup melted butter or margarine
¼ cup blanched almonds
1 teaspoon lemon juice
½ teaspoon salt
⅛ teaspoon pepper

Put all ingredients into blender container in order listed. Cover; blend at medium speed until almonds are chopped. *Makes about ¾ cup.*

Serving Suggestion: Serve hot over fish or seafood.

AIOLI SAUCE ▮

1¼ cups hot milk	1½ tablespoons dry mustard
1 tablespoon cornstarch	¾ teaspoon salt
1 tablespoon softened butter or margarine	⅛ teaspoon pepper
	1 teaspoon vinegar

Put all ingredients into blender container in order listed. Cover; blend at medium speed until smooth. Pour into small saucepan. Cook over medium heat, stirring constantly, until mixture comes to a boil. Reduce heat; simmer 3 minutes. *Makes about 1¼ cups.*

Serving Suggestion: Serve with corned beef, tongue, hamburgers, frankfurters, cold cuts, or fish.

176

MUSTARD SAUCE

2 egg yolks	¼ teaspoon pepper
3 cloves garlic, halved	2 teaspoons lemon juice
¾ teaspoon salt	½ cup olive or vegetable oil

Put egg yolks, garlic, salt, pepper, and 1 teaspoon lemon juice into blender container. Cover; blend at medium speed until garlic is very finely chopped. While blender is running, tip center cap and slowly add ¼ cup oil and remaining lemon juice. Increase speed to high; while blender is running, tip center cap and slowly add remaining oil. *Makes about ¾ cup.*

Serving Suggestion: Serve with lamb, boiled beef, or fish.

ANCHOVY SAUCE ▮

1 cup mayonnaise	1 teaspoon dried dill weed
4 anchovy fillets	

Put all ingredients into blender container in order

listed. Cover; blend at medium speed just until anchovies are chopped. Chill. *Makes 1 cup*.
Serving Suggestion: Serve with veal, fish fillets, or egg dishes.

HORSERADISH CREAM SAUCE

1 slice bread
¼ cup prepared horseradish, drained
1 teaspoon sugar
¼ teaspoon salt
¼ teaspoon prepared mustard (optional)
¼ cup milk
½ cup heavy cream

Tear bread into blender container. Cover; blend at medium speed until bread is crumbed. Add horseradish, sugar, salt, mustard, and milk. Cover; blend at medium speed until thoroughly mixed. Beat heavy cream with electric mixer until stiff. Fold in horseradish mixture. *Makes about 1½ cups*.
Serving Suggestion: Serve with roast beef, corned beef, boiled beef, steak, tongue, ham, or fish.

SPAGHETTI SAUCE WITH MEAT

1 medium onion, cut up
1 clove garlic, halved
4 medium mushrooms
2 tablespoons olive oil
1 pound ground beef
½ cup dry red wine
1 can (about 16 ounces) tomatoes
1 can (6 ounces) tomato paste
¼ cup parsley sprigs
1 teaspoon salt
½ teaspoon dried basil
¼ teaspoon dried oregano
¼ teaspoon pepper

Put onion and garlic into blender container;

cover; ◼ blend at medium speed until chopped. Wipe mushrooms with damp cloth and add to blender container, two at a time; blend until chopped. Heat oil in large saucepan. Add chopped vegetables. Cook over medium heat, stirring occasionally, until onion is transparent. Add meat; cook until lightly browned, breaking up with fork as it cooks. Put remaining ingredients into blender container in order listed. Cover; blend at medium speed until thoroughly mixed. Add to meat mixture; simmer, covered, over low heat 1 hour. If desired, uncover and cook until thickened. *Makes about 4 cups.*

Serving Suggestion: Serve over spaghetti or other pasta.

MARINARA SAUCE

2 tablespoons olive oil	½ cup water
1 large onion, cut up	1½ teaspoons salt
2 cloves garlic, halved	½ teaspoon dried oregano
1 can (about 16 ounces) tomatoes	1 teaspoon dried basil
1 can (6 ounces) tomato paste	¼ teaspoon pepper

Put all ingredients into blender container in order listed. Cover; blend at medium speed until onion is chopped. Pour into saucepan. Cover; simmer 30 minutes. Uncover; simmer 15 to 20 minutes more or until thickened. *Makes about 1 quart.*

Serving Suggestion: Serve over spaghetti, hamburgers, veal cutlets, or seafood.

PESTO SAUCE

¼ cup cubed Parmesan
  cheese
¼ cup cubed Sardo or
  Romano cheese
2 cups cut-up fresh basil
  leaves

2 or 3 tablespoons pine nuts
  (pignoli)
1 clove garlic, halved
½ teaspoon salt
  Dash pepper
1 cup olive oil

Start blender at medium speed. While blender is
running, tip center cap and gradually add cheese,
blending until grated. Empty onto wax paper; set
aside. Put basil leaves, nuts, garlic, salt, and pepper
into blender. Cover; blend at medium speed until
mixture is smooth and pastelike. Add cheese; blend
just until mixed. While blender is running, tip
center cap and add oil in a steady stream; blend
until sauce is consistency of creamed butter. *Makes
enough for 1 pound pasta*.

179

Note: Genuine Pesto Sauce is always made with
fresh basil. If unavailable, you may substitute 1 cup
washed and dried spinach leaves, ½ cup Italian
parsley, and 2 tablespoons dried leaf basil. Pesto
Sauce may be made ahead and stored, covered, in
the refrigerator.

SPANISH SAUCE

1 small onion, cut up
¼ green pepper, seeded and
  cut up
1 can (about 18 ounces)
  tomatoes, drained
2 tablespoons all-purpose flour

2 tablespoons softened
  butter or margarine
1 tablespoon brown sugar
1 teaspoon salt
⅛ teaspoon pepper
  Dash ground cloves

Put onion and green pepper into blender container.
Cover; ◨ blend at medium speed until chopped. Add

remaining ingredients in order listed. Cover; blend at low speed until combined. Pour into saucepan. Cook, stirring constantly, until mixture thickens and comes to a boil. *Makes about 1¾ cups.*

Serving Suggestion: Serve over fish or omelets.

SEAFOOD COCKTAIL SAUCE

¾ cup chili sauce
¼ cup catsup
1 thin slice onion
1 thin slice lemon
1 teaspoon Worcestershire
   sauce
½ teaspoon prepared
   horseradish, drained
Few dashes hot pepper
   sauce

Put all ingredients into blender container in order listed. Cover; blend at medium speed until onion and lemon are chopped and mixture is thoroughly combined. *Makes 1 cup.*

Serving Suggestion: Serve with shrimp, lobster, crab, clams, or other shellfish.

TARTAR SAUCE

5 stuffed green olives
3 parsley sprigs
1 medium dill pickle, cut up
1 thin slice onion
1 tablespoon capers, drained
1 cup mayonnaise
Few dashes hot pepper
   sauce

Start blender at medium speed. While blender is running, tip center cap and add olives; blend until chopped. While blender is still running, add parsley, then pickle, then onion, making sure that each ingredient is chopped before adding next one. Add capers, mayonnaise, and hot pepper sauce. Cover; blend at low speed until thoroughly mixed. *Makes 1¼ cups.*

Serving Suggestion: Serve with fried or broiled fish or shellfish.

SAUCE VERTE (Green Mayonnaise)

10 sprigs watercress, coarse
    stems removed
10 spinach leaves, torn and
    coarse stems removed
  2 tablespoons cut-up fresh
    dill weed, tarragon, or
    chervil sprigs

5 sprigs parsley
1 teaspoon lemon juice
  Dash hot pepper sauce
1 cup mayonnaise

Start blender at high speed. While blender is
running, tip center cap and gradually add
watercress, then spinach, then herbs, blending until
chopped. Add remaining ingredients to blender
container in order listed. Cover; blend at low speed
until combined. *Makes 1¼ cups.*

Serving Suggestions: Serve with cold salmon and
other fish or with vegetable salads.

Note: If fresh herbs are not available, use 1
teaspoon dried herbs, adding to blender with
mayonnaise.

SAUCE REMOULADE

1 hard-cooked egg, shelled
½ clove garlic
1 medium dill pickle, cut up
2 parsley sprigs
1 cup mayonnaise

1 teaspoon dried tarragon
½ teaspoon dry mustard
¼ teaspoon salt
⅛ teaspoon pepper

Start blender at medium speed. While blender is
running, tip center cap and add egg and garlic;
blend until chopped. While blender is still running,
tip center cap and add pickle and parsley; blend
until chopped. Add remaining ingredients in order
listed. Cover; blend at low speed until thoroughly
mixed. *Makes about 1½ cups.*

Serving Suggestion: Serve with shrimp or other
seafood cocktails.

GIBLET GRAVY

¼ cup chicken or turkey
   drippings
¼ cup all-purpose flour
1 cup chicken or turkey
   broth or water
1 cup milk

½ teaspoon salt
Dash pepper
Cooked chicken or turkey
   gizzards, heart, and
   liver, cut up

Put drippings, flour, broth, milk, salt, and pepper into blender container. Cover; blend at medium speed until smooth. Add gizzards, heart, and liver. Blend at medium speed just until chopped. Pour into saucepan (or roasting pan in which poultry was cooked) and cook, stirring constantly, until gravy is thickened. *Makes 2½ cups.*

QUICK MUSHROOM BEEF GRAVY

⅔ cup beef bouillon, or 1
   beef bouillon cube
   dissolved in 1 cup hot
   water
2 tablespoons dry red wine
1 tablespoon all-purpose
   flour

1 tablespoon beef drippings,
   butter, or margarine
1 thin slice onion
¼ teaspoon salt
⅛ teaspoon pepper
1 can (3 or 4 ounces) sliced
   mushrooms, drained

Put all ingredients except mushrooms into blender container in order listed. Cover; blend at medium speed until smooth. Pour into saucepan; add mushrooms. Cook, stirring constantly, until mixture thickens and comes to a boil. *Makes about 1½ cups.*

MARINADE FOR BEEF OR LAMB

¾ cup dry red wine
¾ cup olive or vegetable oil
1 clove garlic, halved
1 thin slice onion

1 teaspoon salt
½ teaspoon dried oregano
½ teaspoon dried basil
⅛ teaspoon pepper

Put all ingredients into blender container in order

listed. Cover; blend at medium speed until onion is chopped. *Makes 1½ cups* (enough for about 6 pounds meat).

Marinade for Fish: Substitute dry white wine for red wine. Proceed as for Marinade for Beef or Lamb. Use to marinate whole fish or fish steaks for baking or grilling.

Serving Suggestions: Use to marinate beef or lamb cubes for shish kebab, flank steak, or shoulder lamb chops, or to baste meat during grilling.

ZESTY BARBECUE SAUCE

1 medium onion, cut up
1 clove garlic, halved
1 thin slice lemon, peeled
¼ cup parsley sprigs
1 bottle (12 ounces) chili sauce
¼ cup wine vinegar

¼ cup vegetable oil
2 teaspoons brown sugar
1 teaspoon Worcestershire sauce
1 teaspoon salt
¼ teaspoon dried thyme
Few dashes hot pepper sauce

Put all ingredients into blender container in order listed. Cover; blend at medium speed until smooth. *Makes 2 cups.*

Serving Suggestion: Brush on chicken, hamburgers or spareribs during grilling.

HONEY-ORANGE GLAZE

½ cup orange juice
½ cup honey

1 cup firmly packed brown sugar
Rind of ¼ orange

Put all ingredients into blender container in order listed. Cover; blend at medium speed until orange rind is finely chopped. *Makes 1½ cups.*

Serving Suggestion: Brush over ham or pork roast during last part of baking or roasting.

Desserts

One of the most popular uses for the blender is in the preparation of desserts. As you browse through the recipes in this chapter, the reason for this will become increasingly clear—how easily and with what variety good desserts are achieved when the blender is put to practical use is truly eye-opening.

It's hard to resist Fresh Applesauce, tart with lemon and blended smooth. Or rich and velvety Chocolate Mousse.

APPLE WALNUT CRISP

1 cup walnuts
5 medium, tart apples, pared, quartered, and cored
1 tablespoon lemon juice
½ cup sugar
½ cup firmly packed brown sugar

½ cup all-purpose flour
¼ teaspoon salt
¼ teaspoon ground cinnamon
¼ cup softened butter or margarine
Whipped cream or ice cream (optional)

Heat oven to 400° F. Put ½ cup walnuts into blender container. Cover; ▮ blend at medium speed until chopped. Empty onto wax paper. Repeat process with remaining nuts; set aside. Cut apple quarters into thirds. Fill blender container to 5-cup mark with apples. Add water to cover apples. Cover; ▮ blend at medium speed just until apples are chopped. Drain thoroughly in sieve. Place half the apples in 9-inch pie plate; sprinkle with half the lemon juice. Repeat with remaining apples and lemon juice. Stir ½ cup sugar into apples. Mix brown sugar, flour, salt, cinnamon, and nuts in small bowl; cut in butter with pastry blender or fork. Sprinkle over apples. Bake 30 minutes or until top is golden brown. Top with whipped cream or ice cream if desired. *Makes 6 servings.*

Opposite: Pears Hélène, page 187.

FRESH APPLESAUCE

½ cup water   ¼ cup sugar
2 tablespoons lemon juice
3 large, tart, green-skinned
    apples

Combine water and lemon juice in large bowl. Core
apples; cut into 1-inch cubes, dropping them into
lemon juice mixture as soon as they are cut. Put
lemon juice mixture with half the apples and the
sugar into blender container. Cover; blend at low
speed until pureed. Turn blender to high speed;
while blender is running, tip center cap and
gradually add remaining apple pieces. Blend until
smooth, adding a little more water if necessary.
Serve at once. *Makes 6 servings*.

186   **Note:** To make Fresh Applesauce with red-skinned
apples, pare apples before cutting into cubes.
Reduce sugar to 3 tablespoons if apples are sweet.
Proceed as for Fresh Applesauce.

Pink Applesauce: Reduce sugar to 3 tablespoons
and add 2 tablespoons red cinnamon candies before
processing. Proceed as for Fresh Applesauce.

Double Applesauce: Substitute apple juice or
cider for water and reduce sugar to 3 tablespoons.
Proceed as for Fresh Applesauce.

Orange Applesauce: Substitute orange juice for
water and reduce sugar to 3 tablespoons. Proceed as
for Fresh Applesauce.

Cooked Applesauce: Prepare Fresh Applesauce.
Pour into saucepan; bring to a boil over medium
heat, stirring constantly. Chill.

PEARS HELENE

2 cups water
3 cups sugar
6 pears with stems, pared
½ cup light cream

3 tablespoons brandy
1 cup semisweet chocolate
pieces

Combine water and sugar in saucepan; bring to
a boil. Add pears; simmer until tender; drain; chill.
Heat cream gently just until heated through. Put
into blender container. Add remaining ingredients to
blender container in order listed. Cover; blend at
high speed until smooth. Place each pear in dessert
dish or individual compote. Top with chocolate
sauce. *Makes 6 servings*.
Note: If chocolate sauce is prepared in advance,
reheat gently to serve.

STEAMED HOLIDAY PUDDING

6 slices dry bread
2 cups seedless raisins
1 cup diced mixed candied
fruits
1 medium apple, pared,
quartered, and cored
1 medium carrot, pared and
cut up
3 thin slices orange
⅓ cup brandy or rum
3 eggs

1 cup dark corn syrup
⅓ cup softened butter or
margarine
2 teaspoons baking powder
1 teaspoon ground
cinnamon
½ teaspoon ground nutmeg
½ teaspoon salt
½ cup all-purpose flour
1 cup walnuts

Break two slices bread into blender container.
Cover; ◧ blend at medium speed until crumbed.
Empty into measuring cup. Repeat process with
remaining bread (you should have 2½ cups crumbs).
Empty into large mixing bowl; stir in raisins and
candied fruits; set aside. Put remaining ingredients
except flour and walnuts into blender container in
order listed. Cover; blend at high speed until

smooth. Add flour and nuts. Cover; blend at
medium speed until nuts are coarsely chopped and
batter is blended. Add to bread crumbs and fruits;
mix thoroughly. Turn into greased and sugared
2-quart mold or heatproof bowl. Cover tightly with
aluminum foil; tie with string. Place on rack in large
kettle. Add enough boiling water to kettle to come
halfway up sides of mold. Cover kettle; steam 4
hours, adding more water as needed. Remove from
kettle; let stand 15 minutes. Unmold. *Makes 12 to
15 servings.*

Note: Pudding may be made ahead. After
steaming, remove cover from mold; cool pudding.
Cover and refrigerate. To reheat, steam 1½ hours.

Serving Suggestion: Serve with Hard Sauce (page
209).

CHOCOLATE MOUSSE

3 squares (1 ounce each) unsweetened chocolate, cut up	2 egg yolks
	½ cup sugar
	Dash salt
½ cup cold milk	1 teaspoon vanilla
2 envelopes unflavored gelatin	1 cup heavy cream
¾ cup scalded milk	1½ cups cracked or crushed ice

Put chocolate into blender container. Cover; ◖ blend
at medium speed until grated. If necessary, turn
blender on and off several times. Add cold milk.
Sprinkle on gelatin; let stand 1 minute. Add scalded
milk. Cover; blend at low speed until gelatin is
dissolved. Add egg yolks, sugar, salt, and vanilla.
Cover; blend at high speed. While blender is
running, tip center cap and gradually add cream;
add ice, blending until smooth. Pour into six dessert
dishes; chill about 15 minutes before serving. Or
pour into 1-quart mold and chill 1 to 2 hours or until
set; unmold. *Makes 6 servings.*

BAVARIAN CREAM

¼ cup cold water
2 envelopes unflavored
    gelatin
¾ cup scalded milk
¼ cup sugar
¼ teaspoon salt

1½ teaspoons vanilla
¼ teaspoon almond extract
1¼ cups cracked or crushed
    ice
1 cup heavy cream

Put cold water into blender container. Sprinkle on gelatin. Let stand 1 minute. Add milk, sugar, and salt. Cover; blend at low speed until gelatin is dissolved. Add vanilla, almond extract, and ice. Cover; blend at high speed. While blender is running, tip center cap and gradually add cream, blending until smooth. Pour into 1-quart mold. Chill until set. Unmold. *Makes 6 to 8 servings.*

Serving Suggestion: Serve with Easy Zabaglione Sauce (page 208) or Melba Sauce (page 208).

Coffee Bavarian Cream: Add 2 tablespoons instant coffee to blender container with gelatin; omit almond extract. Proceed as for Bavarian Cream.

Chocolate Bavarian Cream: Reduce sugar to 2 tablespoons. Add 1 cup semisweet chocolate pieces to blender container after gelatin has been dissolved. Cover; blend at high speed until chocolate is liquefied. Omit almond extract. Proceed as for Bavarian Cream.

QUICK POTS DE CREME

1 package (6 ounces)
    semisweet chocolate
    pieces
1¼ cups light cream, scalded
1 teaspoon instant coffee
    (optional)

2 egg yolks
Dash salt
1 teaspoon vanilla

Put chocolate pieces, cream, and instant coffee if desired into blender container. Cover; blend at high speed until smooth. Add remaining ingredients in order listed. Cover; blend until smooth. Pour into six pots de crème, demitasse or custard cups, or small sherbet glasses. Chill several hours. *Makes 6 servings.*

COFFEE CHARLOTTE RUSSE

½ cup softened butter or
    margarine
1¼ cups confectioners' sugar
4 egg yolks
¼ cup cold strong coffee, or
    ½ teaspoon instant
    coffee dissolved in ¼ cup
    water

12 ladyfingers
Rum or sherry
Whipped cream
Toasted slivered almonds

Put butter, confectioners' sugar, egg yolks, and coffee into blender container. Cover; blend at high speed until smooth. Arrange three ladyfingers in each of four dessert dishes or sherbet glasses; sprinkle with rum or sherry. Spoon coffee mixture into dishes. Chill several hours. Just before serving, top with whipped cream and toasted almonds. *Makes 4 servings.*

BAKED CUSTARD

2 eggs
3 tablespoons sugar
Dash salt

¼ teaspoon vanilla
1½ cups scalded milk
Ground nutmeg

Heat oven to 350° F. Put eggs, sugar, salt, and vanilla into blender container. Cover; blend at low speed until well mixed. Add scalded milk. Cover; blend at low speed until thoroughly mixed. Pour into four 5-ounce custard cups. Place cups in shallow baking pan; pour hot water into pan to depth of 1½ inches. Bake 40 to 45 minutes or until knife inserted in center comes out clean. Sprinkle with nutmeg. *Makes 4 servings.*

VANILLA ICE CREAM

1 tablespoon cold water	½ cup scalded milk
1 teaspoon unflavored gelatin	½ cup sugar
⅛ teaspoon salt	1 teaspoon vanilla
2 egg yolks	1 cup heavy cream, whipped

Put water into blender container. Sprinkle on gelatin. Add salt, egg yolks, and milk. Cover; blend at low speed until smooth. Add sugar and vanilla. Cover; blend at medium speed until smooth. Fold gelatin mixture gently into whipped cream. Pour into freezer tray or shallow pan; freeze until firm. If ice cream is to be kept for later use, cover with foil or plastic wrap. If too solidly frozen to serve, let stand at room temperature until of desired consistency. *Makes 3 cups.*

191

Chocolate Ice Cream: Add one square (1 ounce) unsweetened chocolate, cut up, to blender container with egg yolks; reduce vanilla to ½ teaspoon. Proceed as for Vanilla Ice Cream.

Chocolate Chip Ice Cream: Cut two squares (1 ounce each) semisweet chocolate into quarters. Put into blender container. Cover; ▮ blend at medium speed until grated. Empty onto wax paper. Proceed as for Vanilla Ice Cream, folding chocolate into gelatin mixture with whipped cream.

Strawberry Ice Cream: Reduce vanilla to ½ teaspoon; add 1½ cups strawberries, washed and hulled, to blender container with sugar and vanilla. Proceed as for Vanilla Ice Cream. *Makes 1 quart.*

Peach Ice Cream: Substitute ¼ teaspoon almond extract for vanilla; add 1½ cups peeled, sliced ripe peaches to blender container with sugar and almond extract. Proceed as for Vanilla Ice Cream. *Makes 1 quart.*

Banana Ice Cream: Add 1 tablespoon lemon juice to blender container with water. Reduce sugar to ⅓ cup and vanilla to ½ teaspoon; add 1½ cups sliced bananas to blender container with sugar and vanilla. Proceed as for Vanilla Ice Cream. *Makes 1 quart.*

Butter Pecan Ice Cream: Add 1 tablespoon softened butter to blender container with egg yolks. Substitute ½ cup firmly packed brown sugar for granulated sugar; add ⅓ cup pecans to blender container with brown sugar. Reduce vanilla to ½ teaspoon. Proceed as for Vanilla Ice Cream. *Makes 3⅓ cups.*

Note: For extra flavor, toast pecans before adding.

Biscuit Tortoni: Put ¼ cup toasted blanched almonds into blender container. Cover; ∎ blend at medium speed until chopped. Empty onto wax paper; set aside. Prepare Vanilla Ice Cream, reducing vanilla to ½ teaspoon and adding 1 teaspoon sherry or ¼ teaspoon almond extract. Fold 2 tablespoons chopped almonds into gelatin mixture with whipped cream. Spoon into 3-ounce paper cups. Sprinkle with remaining almonds. Freeze until firm. *Makes 8 to 10 servings.*

CREAMY ORANGE SHERBET

1 cup heavy cream	3 tablespoons sugar
2 thin slices orange, halved	Dash salt
¾ cup orange juice	

Put all ingredients into blender container in order listed. Cover; blend at high speed until smooth.

Pour into freezer tray; freeze until firm. *Makes 4 servings*.

Creamy Pineapple-Orange Sherbet: Substitute pineapple juice for orange juice. Proceed as for Orange Sherbet.

LEMON FRAPPE

1 can (6 ounces) frozen
   lemonade concentrate,
   thawed

¼ cup sugar
4 cups cracked or crushed
   ice

Put all ingredients into blender container in order listed. Cover; blend at high speed until smooth. Serve at once or pour into ice cube tray; cover with plastic wrap; freeze. If frozen too firm to serve, thaw slightly and return to blender container. Cover; blend at high speed until smooth. *Makes 3 to 4 servings*.

Orange Frappé: Substitute one can (6 ounces) frozen orange juice concentrate, thawed, for lemonade. Proceed as for Lemon Frappé.

Lime Frappé: Substitute one can (6 ounces) frozen limeade concentrate, thawed, for lemonade. Proceed as for Lemon Frappé.

193

After Theater Supper for Four
Scalloped Oysters (page 108) or Quiche Lorraine (page 116)
Spinach and Mushroom Salad   Chiffonade Dressing (page 165)
French Rolls
Quick Pots de Creme (page 189)
Coffee

Cookies

You will make cookies more often and in greater variety if your blender is on the counter top day in and day out, ready for action. The blender can simplify all aspects of cookie-making, but it is especially helpful when nuts or fruits need to be chopped or pureed for toppings and fillings.

If you have your own favorite cookie recipe that you have not adapted to the blender technique, all you have to do is find one here that is similar and use that method as a guide.

Homemade cookies, full of nutritious fruits and nuts, milk products, and eggs, are super choices for after-school snacks or a late-evening treat.

Secrets to Successful Cookie-Baking

Follow recipes carefully for order of adding ingredients and timing.

Use shiny aluminum cookie sheets. Dark ones absorb heat, resulting in cookies that are overbrowned.

Bake only one sheet of cookies at a time in the oven and place it on a rack in the upper third of the oven. If you must bake two sheets at a time, place the second rack just above or below the first rack and stagger the cookie sheets so that one isn't directly above or under the other. Then reverse the position of the sheets halfway through the baking time for even browning.

Cool the cookie sheet before placing another batch on it—hot cookie sheets can spoil the shape of cookies to be baked.

Transfer baked cookies to a wire rack for cooling.

Storing Cookies Properly

To store soft cookies, allow them to cool thoroughly. Then place them in a container—cookie jar or tin—with a tight-fitting lid. A piece of apple, orange, or bread placed in the cookie jar will help to prevent cookies from drying out. Replace it often. Store bar cookies right in the baking pan, tightly covered. To store crisp cookies, allow them to cool and then place them in a container with a loose-fitting cover. If they soften, crisp them in a 300° F. oven for about 5 minutes before serving.

Opposite: Sugar Cookies, page 199; Macaroons, page 198.

195

CHOCOLATE BUTTERSCOTCH COOKIES

¾ cup pecans
½ cup semisweet chocolate
  pieces
½ cup butterscotch pieces
½ cup softened butter or
  margarine
½ cup sugar
¼ cup firmly packed brown
  sugar

1 egg
1 teaspoon vanilla
1 cup sifted all-purpose
  flour
½ teaspoon baking soda
½ teaspoon salt

Heat oven to 375° F. Put pecans into blender container. Cover; ▮ blend at medium speed until chopped. Empty into mixing bowl; add chocolate and butterscotch pieces. Put remaining ingredients into blender container in order listed. Cover; blend at high speed until smooth. If necessary, stop blender during processing and push ingredients toward blades with rubber spatula. Empty into bowl with nut mixture; mix well. Drop by teaspoonfuls, 2 inches apart, onto greased cookie sheets. Bake 10 to 12 minutes or until lightly browned. Cool on cookie sheets 1 minute. Transfer to wire racks with spatula; cool. *Makes 3½ dozen.*

PEANUT DROPS

1½ cups salted peanuts
1 egg
½ cup sugar

¼ teaspoon vanilla
2 teaspoons all-purpose
  flour

Heat oven to 350° F. Put half the peanuts into blender container. Cover; ▮ blend at medium speed

until coarsely chopped. Empty onto wax paper.
Repeat process with remaining peanuts; set aside.
Put remaining ingredients into blender container in
order listed. Cover; blend at medium speed until
thoroughly combined. If necessary, stop blender
during processing and push ingredients toward
blades with rubber spatula. Add peanuts. Cover;
blend until well mixed. Drop by teaspoonfuls, 2
inches apart, onto greased cookie sheets. Bake 10 to
12 minutes. Cool on cookie sheets 1 minute.
Transfer to wire racks with spatula; cool. *Makes 2½
to 3 dozen.*

Lunchbox Fare
Bologna and Cheese Spread Sandwich (page 45)
Carrot Strips
Apple Oatmeal Cookies (page 197)
Banana
Milk

APPLE OATMEAL COOKIES

1½ cups sifted all-purpose flour	1 egg
1 teaspoon baking powder	1 cup sugar
½ teaspoon baking soda	½ cup soft shortening
1½ cups rolled oats	1 teaspoon salt
¼ cup milk	1 teaspoon ground cinnamon
2 medium apples, pared, quartered, and cored	½ teaspoon ground nutmeg
¾ cup seedless raisins	¼ teaspoon ground cloves
	1 cup pecans

Have all ingredients at room temperature. Sift flour,
baking powder, and baking soda into large mixing
bowl. Stir in rolled oats; set aside. Put milk into
blender container. Cover; start blender at medium
speed. Tip center cap; gradually add apple pieces
and raisins, blending until finely chopped. Add egg,

sugar, shortening, salt, and spices. Cover; blend at medium speed until well mixed. If necessary, stop blender during processing and push ingredients toward blades with rubber spatula. Add pecans. Cover; blend at medium speed until nuts are coarsely chopped. Pour over dry ingredients; mix well. Chill 1 to 2 hours. Heat oven to 375° F. Drop dough by teaspoonfuls, 2 inches apart, onto greased cookie sheets. Bake 15 minutes or until lightly browned. Cool 1 minute on cookie sheets. Transfer to wire racks with spatula. Cool. *Makes about 5 dozen*.

SOUR CREAM ORANGE DROPS

1 egg	1 cup seedless raisins
¼ cup orange juice	½ cup pecans
½ cup sour cream	2 cups sifted all-purpose
½ cup softened butter or	flour
margarine	½ teaspoon baking soda
¾ cup sugar	1 teaspoon salt

Have all ingredients at room temperature. Heat oven to 375° F. Put egg, orange juice, sour cream, butter, and sugar into blender container. Cover; blend at medium speed until smooth. Add raisins and pecans. Cover; blend at medium speed until chopped. Sift flour, baking soda, and salt into mixing bowl. Add blended mixture; mix well. Drop by teaspoonfuls, 2 inches apart, onto greased cookie sheets. Bake 10 minutes or until lightly browned. Cool 1 minute on cookie sheets. Transfer to wire racks with spatula; cool. *Makes 4 dozen*.

MACAROONS

2 cups moist shredded	10 candied cherries
coconut	1 teaspoon almond extract
½ cup sweetened condensed	9 candied cherries halved
milk	

Heat oven to 325° F. Put 1 cup coconut into blender container. Cover; ∎blend at low speed until chopped. Empty into bowl. Put condensed milk, remaining 1 cup coconut, 10 cherries, and almond extract into blender container. Cover; blend at high speed until cherries are chopped. Add to chopped coconut; mix well. Drop by tablespoonfuls, 2 inches apart, onto lightly greased cookie sheets. Top each cookie with ½ candied cherry. Bake 15 minutes or until lightly browned around edges. Cool on cookie sheets 5 minutes. Transfer to wire racks with spatula. Cool. *Makes about 1½ dozen.*

Note: For bite-size macaroons, drop by teaspoonfuls, 1 inch apart. Bake 10 minutes or until lightly browned around edges. *Makes about 3 dozen.*

SUGAR COOKIES

2½ cups sifted all-purpose flour	¼ cup milk
2½ teaspoons baking powder	1 tablespoon lemon juice
¼ teaspoon salt	¾ cup sugar
Rind of ½ lemon	1 cup softened butter or margarine

Have all ingredients at room temperature. Sift flour, baking powder, and salt into large mixing bowl. Put lemon rind into blender container. Cover; blend at low speed until very finely chopped. Put remaining ingredients into blender container in order listed. Cover; blend at high speed until smooth. Add blended mixture to dry ingredients; mix thoroughly. Chill dough at least 1 hour. Heat oven to 400° F. Work with a quarter of dough at a time, keeping remainder refrigerated. Roll dough out on lightly floured board until very thin. Cut with small, floured cookie cutters. If desired, sprinkle lightly with additional sugar. Place, 2 inches apart, on ungreased cookie sheets. Bake about 8 minutes or until edges are lightly browned. Cool 1 minute on cookie sheets. Transfer to wire racks with spatula; cool. *Makes 4 to 5 dozen.*

CREAM CHEESE CRISPS

1½ cups cornflakes
1 cup sifted all-purpose flour
2 teaspoons baking powder
½ teaspoon salt
⅓ cup softened butter or margarine

1 package (3 ounces) cream cheese, cubed and softened
½ cup sugar
1 teaspoon lemon juice

Have all ingredients at room temperature. Heat oven to 375° F. Put half the cornflakes into blender container. Cover; blend at medium speed until finely crumbed. Empty onto wax paper. Repeat process with remaining cornflakes. Sift flour, baking powder, and salt into mixing bowl. Put remaining ingredients into blender container in order listed. Cover; blend at high speed until smooth. If necessary, stop blender during processing and push ingredients toward blades with rubber spatula. Add blended mixture to dry ingredients; mix well. Shape dough into small balls. Roll in cornflake crumbs. Place, 2 inches apart, on ungreased cookie sheets; flatten with fork. Bake 15 minutes or until lightly browned. Cool 1 minute on cookie sheets. Transfer to wire racks with spatula; cool. *Makes 3 dozen.*

200

CHOCOLATE BROWNIES

2 eggs
2 squares (1 ounce each) unsweetened chocolate, cut up
¼ cup soft shortening

1 cup sugar
½ cup sifted all-purpose flour
¼ teaspoon salt
½ cup walnuts or pecans

Heat oven to 350° F. Grease 8 x 8 x 2-inch pan. Put eggs, chocolate, shortening, and sugar into blender container. Cover; blend at high speed until smooth.

Add flour and salt. Cover; blend at medium speed just until mixed. If necessary, stop blender during processing and push ingredients toward blades with rubber spatula. Add nuts. Cover; blend at medium speed just until nuts are chopped. Spread evenly in prepared pan. Bake 35 minutes or until top has dull crust. Cool slightly. Cut into 2-inch squares. *Makes 16.*

NO-BAKE COCONUT RUM BALLS

1 box (12 ounces) vanilla
    wafers
1 cup walnuts
1 can (3½ ounces) flaked
    coconut
1 can (14 ounces) sweetened
    condensed milk

¼ cup rum
Sifted confectioners' sugar
Additional coconut or
    chopped nuts (optional)

Break six to eight vanilla wafers into blender container. Cover; blend at medium speed until crumbed. Empty into mixing bowl. Repeat process with remaining wafers. Put walnuts into blender container. Cover; ⊓ blend at medium speed until chopped. Add to wafer crumbs. Add coconut, condensed milk, and rum; mix well. Chill several hours or overnight. Dip palms of hands in confectioners' sugar; pinch off portions of chilled mixture. Roll into 1-inch balls. If mixture becomes too soft, return to refrigerator and chill. If desired, roll balls in additional coconut. Store covered in refrigerator. *Makes about 2½ dozen.*

Watching the Game on T.V.
Cheese Fondue (page 115)   French Bread Chunks
Chicken Curry with Condiments (page 96)
Rice
Vegetable Relishes—Carrots, Celery, Olives
Peanut Drops (page 196)   Macaroons (page 198)
Coffee

Frostings, Glazes, Toppings, Dessert Sauces, and Syrups

Putting the frosting on the cake, pouring the sauce on the pudding, topping a dessert, or glazing a pretty pastry ... these are the final touches that make a dessert truly special, adding to its eye appeal, as well as giving it that extra flavor. The "final touches" that follow here are designed for your blender to make quick work of. And best of all, they'll be every bit as good as you imagined, either smooth and velvety or fine and crunchy.

VANILLA BUTTER-CREAM FROSTING

1 egg white	1 teaspoon vanilla
6 tablespoons softened butter or margarine	Dash salt
2 tablespoons hot milk	3½ cups sifted confectioners' sugar

Put egg white, butter, hot milk, vanilla, salt, and 1 cup confectioners' sugar into blender container. Cover; blend at high speed until smooth. Gradually add remaining confectioners' sugar, blending until smooth. If necessary, stop blender during processing and push ingredients toward blades with rubber spatula. *Makes enough to fill and frost two 8 or 9-inch cake layers.*

Coffee Butter-Cream Frosting: Put 1 tablespoon instant coffee into blender container before adding confectioners' sugar. Rum extract or brandy flavoring may be used in place of vanilla. Proceed as for Vanilla Butter-Cream Frosting.

Opposite: Peach Melba, page 209.

CHOCOLATE BUTTER-CREAM FROSTING

3 squares (1 ounce each)
    unsweetened chocolate,
    cut up
½ cup hot milk
3½ cups sifted confectioners'
    sugar

1 egg yolk
6 tablespoons softened
    butter or margarine
1 teaspoon vanilla
Dash salt

204 Put chocolate into blender container. Cover; ◖ blend
at medium speed until grated. Add milk. Cover;
blend at high speed until smooth. Add 1 cup
confectioners' sugar and remaining ingredients in
order listed. Cover; blend at high speed until
smooth. Gradually add remaining confectioners'
sugar, blending until smooth. If necessary, stop
blender during processing and push ingredients
toward blades with rubber spatula. *Makes enough to
fill and frost two 8 or 9-inch cake layers.*

CREAMY WHITE FROSTING

¼ cup light cream
1 teaspoon vanilla
1 package (3 ounces) cream
    cheese, cubed and
    softened

2 teaspoons softened butter
    or margarine
½ teaspoon salt
3 cups sifted confectioners'
    sugar

Put cream, vanilla, cream cheese, butter, and salt into blender container. Cover; blend at low speed until smooth. Add 1 cup confectioners' sugar. Cover; blend at high speed until smooth. Gradually add remaining confectioners' sugar, blending until smooth. If necessary, stop blender during processing and push ingredients toward blades with rubber spatula. *Makes enough to fill and frost two 8 or 9-inch cake layers.*

LADY BALTIMORE FROSTING

⅓ cup seedless raisins	¼ teaspoon cream of tartar
⅓ cup candied cherries	⅓ cup cold water
⅓ cup pecans	Dash salt
4 dried figs, cut up	1 teaspoon vanilla
2 egg whites	2 white cake layers
1½ cups sugar	

Put raisins, cherries, pecans, and figs into blender container. Cover; blend at medium speed until chopped. If necessary, turn blender on and off several times. Empty into mixing bowl; set aside. Put egg whites, sugar, cream of tartar, water, and salt into top of double boiler. Beat with electric mixer to blend. Place over boiling water. Cook, beating constantly, about 7 minutes or until stiff peaks form. Remove from heat; beat in vanilla. Combine ½ cup frosting with chopped fruits and nuts. Use as cake filling. Spread remaining frosting on top and sides of white cake. *Makes enough to fill and frost two 8 or 9-inch cake layers.*

Fluffy White Frosting: Omit fruits and nuts. Proceed as for Lady Baltimore Frosting.

CHOCOLATE GLAZE

2 squares (1 ounce each)
unsweetened chocolate,
cut up
¼ cup softened butter or
margarine

½ teaspoon vanilla
Dash salt
⅓ cup boiling water
2 cups sifted confectioners'
sugar

Put chocolate into blender container. Cover; ◖ blend
at medium speed until grated. Add butter, vanilla,
salt, and boiling water. Cover; blend at high speed
until smooth. Add confectioners' sugar. Cover;
blend at low speed until smooth. If necessary, stop
blender during processing and push ingredients
toward blades with rubber spatula. Use
immediately. *Makes about ¾ cup.*

Serving Suggestion: Use to glaze angel food or
chiffon cakes, brownies, or other bar cookies.

CHOCOLATE-COCONUT TOPPING

1½ cups semisweet chocolate
pieces
6 tablespoons boiling water

2 cups moist shredded
coconut

Put chocolate pieces and boiling water into blender
container. Cover; blend at high speed until smooth.
Add coconut. Cover; blend at medium speed until
coconut is chopped. If necessary, stop blender
during processing and push ingredients toward
blades with rubber spatula. *Enough to top one 13 x
9 x 2-inch cake.*

Serving Suggestion: Sprinkle over white or
yellow cake while cake is still warm.

BLENDER WHIPPED CREAM

Pour 1 cup chilled heavy cream into blender
container. Cover; blend at low speed just until
cream thickens and begins to hold the shape of the

blades. Remove cover during whipping so that you can watch carefully, as overblending will quickly turn cream to butter. *Makes 1¼ cups*.

Note: To whip more than 1 cup of cream, repeat blender process after cleaning blender container.

Sweetened Whipped Cream: To each 1 cup heavy cream, add 1 to 2 tablespoons sugar and ½ teaspoon vanilla before blending.

Cocoa Whipped Cream: To each 1 cup heavy cream, add 2 tablespoons cocoa and 3 tablespoons confectioners' sugar before blending.

Mocha Whipped Cream: To each 1 cup heavy cream, add 2 tablespoons cocoa, ¼ cup confectioners' sugar, and 1 teaspoon instant coffee before blending.

Lemon Whipped Cream: To each 1 cup heavy cream, add ½ cup confectioners' sugar, 1 tablespoon lemon juice, and a small piece of lemon rind before blending.

Brandied Whipped Cream: To each 1 cup heavy cream, add 3 tablespoons confectioners' sugar and 2 tablespoons brandy before blending.

HOT FUDGE SAUCE

3 squares (1 ounce each) unsweetened chocolate, cut up	½ cup hot milk ¾ cup sugar 1 teaspoon vanilla

Put chocolate pieces into blender container. Cover; ◙ blend at medium speed until grated. Add hot milk, sugar, and vanilla. Cover; blend at high speed until smooth. If necessary, stop blender during processing and push ingredients toward blades with rubber spatula. Use immediately. *Makes about 1 cup*.

Note: To serve leftover sauce, reheat gently.

BUTTERSCOTCH SAUCE 🧂

½ cup evaporated milk
¾ cup firmly packed brown
    sugar
¼ cup sugar

1 tablespoon light corn
    syrup
1 teaspoon vanilla
¼ teaspoon rum extract

Put all ingredients into blender container in order listed. Cover; blend at high speed until smooth. *Makes about 1 cup*.

EASY ZABAGLIONE SAUCE

1 cup cold milk
1½ cups light cream
1 package (4-serving size)
    vanilla flavor instant
    pudding mix

1 egg white
2 tablespoons sugar
¼ cup sherry or Marsala
    wine

Put milk, cream, and pudding mix into blender container. Cover; blend at low speed until smooth. Beat egg white in medium mixing bowl with electric mixer until foamy; gradually beat in sugar; continue beating until stiff but not dry. Fold pudding mixture into egg white. Chill. Just before serving, gently stir in wine. *Makes about 2¾ cups*.

Serving Suggestion: Use to top Bavarian Cream (page 189), fruit, pound cake, etc.

MELBA SAUCE

1 package (10 ounces)
    frozen raspberries,
    thawed

1 tablespoon orange-
    flavored liqueur
1 teaspoon lemon juice

Put all ingredients into blender container in order listed. Cover; blend at low speed until pureed. Strain to remove seeds. Chill. *Makes about 1¼ cups*.

Serving Suggestion: Use to top peach halves and

vanilla ice cream, custards, puddings, or other desserts.

Peach Melba: Fill peach halves with vanilla ice cream and top with Melba Sauce.

HARD SAUCE

2 tablespoons rum or brandy	2 cups sifted confectioners' sugar
2 tablespoons heavy cream or milk	½ cup softened butter or margarine

Put rum, cream, and 1 cup confectioners' sugar into blender container. Cover; blend at high speed until smooth. Add butter and remaining confectioners' sugar. Cover; blend at high speed until smooth. If necessary, stop blender during processing and push ingredients toward blades with rubber spatula. *Makes 1 cup.*

209

BLUEBERRY SYRUP

1 can (1 pound) blueberries with syrup	½ cup light corn syrup
	⅛ teaspoon salt

Put all ingredients into blender container in order listed. Cover; blend at high speed until smooth. Pour into saucepan. Bring to a boil. Cook over moderate heat, stirring constantly, for 5 minutes. Use warm or chilled. *Makes about 2 cups.*

Christmas Eve Dinner
Broiled Stuffed Mushrooms (page 36)
Olive-Filled Cheese Balls (page 36)
Blanquette de Veau (page 83)   Buttered Noodles
Tomatoes Provençal (page 129)
Crisp Green Salad   Cloverleaf Rolls (page 143)
Steamed Holiday Pudding (page 187)   Hard Sauce (page 209)
Coffee

Pies, Pastry, and Cakes

A bright new world of pastry delights, from heavenly chiffons to robust chocolate concoctions, is yours—with the help of your blender. Of all the delicious meal-ending possibilities, there is perhaps none that can show off your culinary accomplishments as well as a luscious, mouth-watering pie with a flaky, tender, melt-in-your-mouth pastry.

Just as you can count on at least one member of the family—not to mention a whole host of friends—to name pie or cake as a favorite dessert, you can rely on your blender to help you create these favorites.

Secrets to Making Pies and Pastry

Measure ingredients for pastry and fillings accurately to ensure perfect results.

Handle pastry delicately—too much handling will toughen it. For golden brown two-crust pies, brush the top crust with milk or cream; for a festive touch, sprinkle it with sugar. Crush cookies and crackers in blender to make crumbs for crumb crusts. (See page 14.)

To help prevent soggy bottom crusts in pumpkin and custard pies, reserve 1 teaspoonful of beaten egg and brush over pastry crust; chill, then add filling.

Pastry and crumb crusts may be made ahead and frozen if desired.

Cook fillings for cream pies in a heavy saucepan and stir constantly to prevent scorching.

Avoid overcooking filling that has a cornstarch base to prevent thinning the filling.

Refrigerate chiffon, custard, and cream pies and those with whipped cream toppings.

To chill chiffon pies quickly, place saucepan containing filling in a large pan or bowl filled with ice cubes and water. Stir filling until mixture begins to thicken and mounds when spooned. Remove from chilled water immediately and quickly fold in any remaining ingredients.

211

Opposite: Lemon Chiffon Pie, page 216.

PASTRY CRUST (For one-crust pie)

1 cup sifted all-purpose
    flour
¼ teaspoon salt

⅓ cup soft shortening
2 tablespoons cold water

Sift flour with salt into mixing bowl. Cut in
shortening with pastry blender until mixture
resembles cornmeal. Sprinkle water evenly over
surface. Stir with fork until all dry particles are
moistened and pastry clings together. Shape into
ball. Roll out on floured surface to 12-inch circle;
fold in half. Lift carefully into 9-inch pie plate;
unfold. Do not stretch pastry. Fold under excess
pastry until even with edge of pie plate. Pinch with
fingers to form a high, standing collar all around
rim. Flute edge as desired.

Unbaked Pastry Crust: When filling and crust
are to be baked together, follow time and
temperature requirements of filling recipe.

Baked Pastry Crust: Heat oven to 450° F.
Prepare Standard Pastry, line pie plate, and flute
edge as above. Prick bottom and sides of pastry
thoroughly with fork. Fit a piece of wax paper or
aluminum foil into pastry shell. Fill with raw rice or
dried beans to prevent pastry from bubbling and
shrinking until it sets. Bake 8 to 10 minutes.
Remove rice or beans and paper or foil. Bake shell 8
to 10 minutes longer or until golden brown. Cool
before filling.

Cheese Pastry (for one-crust pie): Put ½ cup
cubed Cheddar cheese into blender container.
Cover; ◨ blend at medium speed until grated. Add
cheese to flour mixture with shortening and increase
water to 4 tablespoons. Proceed as for Pastry Crust.

Nut Pastry (for one-crust pie): Put ½ cup walnuts

or pecans into blender container. Cover; blend at medium speed until ground. Add to flour-salt mixture. Proceed as for Pastry Crust.

GRAHAM CRACKER CRUST

14 graham crackers
¼ cup sugar
¼ teaspoon ground cinnamon

¼ cup melted butter or margarine

Break seven graham crackers into blender container. Cover; blend at medium speed until crumbed. Empty into bowl. Repeat process with remaining crackers. Stir sugar, cinnamon, and melted butter into crumbs until thoroughly combined. Press onto bottom and sides of 9-inch pie plate. Chill.

Chocolate Graham Cracker Crust: Put one square (1 ounce) unsweetened chocolate, cut up, into blender container. Cover; blend at medium speed until finely grated. Stir into crumbs. Proceed as for Graham Cracker Crust.

Vanilla or Chocolate Crumb Crust: Substitute thirty-six vanilla wafers or twenty-seven chocolate wafers for graham crackers; reduce sugar to 2 tablespoons. Proceed as for Graham Cracker Crust.

NUT CRUST

1½ cups walnuts or pecans
3 tablespoons sugar

⅓ cup melted butter or margarine

Put ½ cup nuts into blender container. Cover; blend at medium speed until ground. Empty onto wax paper. Repeat process with remaining nuts. Stir

sugar and ground nuts into melted butter until
thoroughly combined. Press firmly onto bottom and
sides of 9-inch pie plate. Chill.

PUMPKIN PIE

1 can (13 ounces)
 evaporated milk
1 can (1 pound) pumpkin
2 eggs
½ cup sugar
¼ cup firmly packed brown
 sugar

1 teaspoon ground
 cinnamon
½ teaspoon ground nutmeg
¼ teaspoon ground ginger
⅛ teaspoon ground cloves
½ teaspoon salt
9-inch unbaked Pastry Crust
 (page 212)

214 Heat oven to 425° F. Put all ingredients except
Pastry Crust into blender container in order listed.
Cover; blend at medium speed until thoroughly
mixed. Pour into pastry crust. Bake 15 minutes.
Reduce oven temperature to 325° F. Bake 45
minutes or until thin-bladed knife inserted 1 inch
from edge comes out clean. Cool. *Makes one 9-inch
pie*.

Pumpkin-Pecan Pie: Put ½ cup pecans into
blender container. Cover; ◼ blend at medium speed
until chopped. Combine chopped nuts, ¼ cup firmly
packed brown sugar, and ¼ cup melted butter or
margarine. Prepare Pumpkin Pie. Sprinkle with nut
mixture after 25 minutes of baking. Proceed to bake
as for Pumpkin Pie.

PECAN PIE

3 eggs
¼ cup softened butter or
   margarine
¼ cup sugar
1 cup dark corn syrup

1 teaspoon vanilla
1½ cups pecans
9-inch unbaked Pastry Crust
   (page 212)
Whipped cream (optional)

Heat oven to 350° F. Put eggs, butter, sugar, corn
syrup, and vanilla into blender container. Cover;
blend at medium speed about 2 minutes or until
very light and fluffy. Add pecans. Cover; blend at
medium speed just until nuts are coarsely chopped.
Pour into pastry crust. Bake 40 to 50 minutes or
until filling is set at edges but is still slightly soft in
center (overbaking will cause filling to curdle). Cool.
Top with whipped cream if desired. *Makes one
9-inch pie.*

215

Walnut Pie: Substitute walnuts for pecans.
Proceed as for Pecan Pie.

BANANA CREAM PIE

1½ cups milk
1 package (6-serving size)
   instant vanilla pudding
3 medium bananas
9-inch Baked Pastry Crust
   (page 212) or Vanilla
   Crumb Crust (page 213)

Whipped cream and
   banana slices (optional)

Put milk and pudding mix into blender container.
Cover; blend at medium speed until mixed. Slice
bananas into pastry or crumb crust. Pour pudding
over bananas. Chill until set. Garnish with whipped
cream and banana slices if desired. *Makes one
9-inch pie.*

LEMON CHIFFON PIE

¼ cup cold water
1 envelope unflavored
  gelatin
½ cup boiling water
¾ cup sugar
¼ cup lemon juice
1 thin slice lemon

¼ teaspoon salt
9-inch Baked Pastry Crust
  (page 212) or Graham
  Cracker Crust (page 213)
  Whipped cream (optional)
1 thin slice lemon

Put cold water into blender container. Sprinkle on gelatin; let stand 1 minute. Add boiling water and ½ cup sugar. Cover; blend at low speed until gelatin and sugar are dissolved. Add lemon juice and 1 lemon slice. Cover; blend at medium speed until lemon is very finely chopped. Add egg yolks and salt. Cover; blend at high speed until thoroughly mixed. Pour into large bowl. Chill until mixture mounds when spooned. Beat egg whites with electric mixer until foamy; gradually beat in remaining ¼ cup sugar; continue beating until stiff but not dry. Fold gently into lemon mixture. Turn into crust. Chill until set. Top with whipped cream if desired. Garnish with lemon twist. *Makes one 9-inch pie.*

KEY LIME PIE

1 package (4-serving size)
  lime-flavor gelatin
  Rind of ¼ lime, cut up
½ cup boiling water
½ cup lime juice
2 eggs, separated
1 can (14 ounces) sweetened
  condensed milk

1 teaspoon aromatic bitters
  (optional)
9-inch baked Pastry Crust
  (page 212) or Graham
  Cracker Crust (page 213)

Put gelatin and lime rind into blender container. Add boiling water. Cover; blend at medium speed until gelatin is dissolved and rind is finely chopped. Add lime juice and egg yolks. Cover; blend at medium speed until thoroughly mixed. Add condensed milk and bitters. Cover; blend at medium speed until mixed. Beat egg whites with electric mixer until stiff but not dry. Fold gently into lime mixture. Turn into crust. Chill until set. *Makes one 9-inch pie.*

Key Lime Tarts: Substitute individual tarts for Pastry Crust or Graham Cracker Crust. Proceed as for Key Lime Pie.

GRAHAM-NUT TORTE

14 graham crackers
1 cup sifted cake flour
¾ teaspoon salt
2 teaspoons baking powder
1 cup milk
2 eggs
¾ cup sugar
1 teaspoon vanilla
½ cup soft shortening
1 cup pecans

Heat oven to 350° F. Grease 9 x 9 x 2-inch pan. Break seven graham crackers into blender container. Cover; ⬛ blend at medium speed until crumbed. Empty into mixing bowl. Repeat process with remaining crackers (you should have 1 cup crumbs); set aside. Sift flour, salt, and baking powder into bowl with crumbs; mix well. Put milk, eggs, sugar, vanilla, and shortening into blender container. Cover; blend at high speed until smooth. Add pecans. Cover; blend at medium speed just until pecans are chopped. Add to dry ingredients; mix lightly. Pour into prepared pan. Bake 30 minutes or until cake tests done. Serve warm. *Makes one 9-inch square torte.*

Serving Suggestion: Top with Hard Sauce (page 209) or whipped cream.

GREEK NUT CAKE

Cake:
- 2 cups walnuts
- 2¼ cups sifted all-purpose flour
- 2½ teaspoons baking powder
- ½ cup softened butter or margarine
- 1 cup sugar
- 3 eggs
- ⅓ cup milk
- ¼ teaspoon ground cloves
- ¼ teaspoon salt
- 1 teaspoon ground cinnamon

Honey Syrup:
- ¾ cup sugar
- ¼ cup honey
- 1 tablespoon lemon juice
- 1 cup boiling water

Prepare Cake: Heat oven to 350° F. Grease and flour 10-inch round or fluted tube pan. Put ½ cup walnuts into blender container. Cover; ⊞ blend at medium speed until ground. Empty into large mixing bowl. Repeat process with remaining walnuts, ½ cup at a time. Sift flour and baking powder into bowl with nuts. Put butter, sugar, eggs, milk, cinnamon, cloves, and salt into blender container. Cover; blend at high speed until smooth. Add to flour-nut mixture; combine thoroughly. Pour into prepared pan. Bake 40 minutes or until cake tests done.

Prepare Honey Syrup: Put sugar, honey, lemon juice, and water into blender container. Cover; blend at high speed until smooth. When cake is done, allow it to cool 10 minutes; remove from pan. Prick surface deeply in several places with tines of fork. Baste several times with Honey Syrup until cake is soaked and all syrup is used. *Makes one 10-inch round or tube cake.*

218

CHEESECAKE

Graham Cracker Crust
(page 213)
3 eggs
½ cup sugar
1 teaspoon vanilla

1 thin strip lemon rind
1 cup sour cream
1 package (8 ounces) cream
cheese, cubed and
softened

Reserve 2 tablespoons Graham Cracker Crust mixture for topping. Press remaining mixture into bottom and about 2 inches up sides of greased 8-inch springform or round layer-cake pan at least 2½ inches deep. Chill thoroughly. Heat oven to 325° F. Put eggs, sugar, vanilla, lemon rind, and sour cream into blender container. Cover; blend at high speed about 10 seconds. While blender is running, tip center cap and add cream cheese gradually; blend until smooth. If necessary, stop blender during processing and push ingredients toward blades with rubber spatula. Pour into crumb-lined pan. Sprinkle reserved 2 tablespoons crumb mixture over top. Bake about 55 minutes or until set in center. Filling will be soft but will firm as cake cools. Store in refrigerator. *Makes one 8-inch cake.*

Pineapple Cheesecake: Thoroughly drain one can (8¼ ounces) crushed pineapple and add to smooth cream cheese mixture in blender container; blend 5 seconds longer. Pour into prepared pan and bake as for Cheesecake.

Quick Fruit-Glazed Cheesecake: Top cooled cheesecake with your favorite canned fruit pie filling, such as cherry, peach, or blueberry.

Preserves and Relishes

In a time when the supermarket has replaced the traditional family food cellar, few people bother to do much large-scale pickling or preserving any longer. However, with today's resurgence of interest in vegetable gardening, many people are deriving great pleasure from using their homegrowns in the creation of superlative relishes and jams, though perhaps not in the large quantities that marked the canning habits of our forebears. These homemade treats make not only tasty contributions to family tables for everyday dining and entertaining but also splendid hostess or holiday gifts and bazaar offerings.

The recipes that follow have been carefully selected to justify that little bit of extra effort involved in making your own preserves and relishes. All the hard work is done by the blender, and the results are sure to bring both satisfaction and compliments to the cook!

QUICK CORN RELISH

2 cups vinegar
1 tablespoon dry mustard
1 tablespoon celery seeds
1 tablespoon salt
1¼ cups firmly packed light
   brown sugar
1 small green pepper,
   seeded and cut up

¼ sweet red pepper, seeded
   and cut up
1 large onion, cut up
4 cups cooked or canned
   corn, drained

Put all ingredients except corn into blender container. Cover; blend at medium speed until vegetables are chopped. Pour into large saucepan; add corn. Bring to a boil; reduce heat; simmer, uncovered, 20 minutes. Pour into hot, sterilized pint jars. Seal at once. *Makes 4 pints*.

Opposite: Sweet Pepper Relish, page 222.

SWEET PEPPER RELISH

12 medium green peppers, seeded and cut up	Boiling water
12 medium sweet red peppers, seeded and cut up	2 cups cider vinegar
	1¾ cups sugar
	1 tablespoon salt
4 medium onions, cut up	1 teaspoon mustard seeds

Fill blender container to 5-cup mark with cut-up vegetables. Add cold water to cover vegetables. Cover; ◧ blend at medium speed just until vegetables are chopped. Drain thoroughly in colander; return any large pieces to blender container. Empty vegetables from colander into large saucepan. Repeat procedure until all vegetables are chopped. Pour boiling water over vegetables in saucepan to cover; let stand 15 minutes. Drain in colander 4 to 5 hours. Return vegetables to saucepan. Add vinegar, sugar, salt, and mustard seeds. Heat to boiling; reduce heat; simmer, uncovered, 20 minutes. Ladle into hot, sterilized pint jars. Seal at once. *Makes 4½ pints.*

QUICK GARDEN RELISH

½ medium head green cabbage, coarsely cut up	¾ cup cider vinegar
2 carrots, pared and cut up	¾ cup sugar
1 green pepper, seeded and cut up	2 teaspoons salt
	½ teaspoon mustard seeds
1 medium onion, cut up	½ teaspoon celery seeds

Fill blender container to 5-cup mark with cut-up vegetables. Add cold water to cover vegetables. Cover; ◧ blend at medium speed just until vegetables are chopped. Drain thoroughly in colander; return any large pieces to blender container. Empty vegetables from colander into bowl. Repeat procedure until all vegetables are chopped. Put remaining ingredients into blender container in order listed. Cover; blend at low speed until mixed. Pour over chopped vegetables; mix well. Refrigerate at least 2 hours before serving. *Makes about 5 cups.*

HORSERADISH-BEET RELISH

1 tablespoon vinegar	⅛ teaspoon pepper
1 tablespoon sugar	1 teaspoon salt
1 can (16 ounces) diced beets, drained	¼ cup prepared horseradish drained

Put all ingredients into blender container in order listed. Cover; blend at medium speed just until beets are finely chopped. Refrigerate 2 to 3 days. *Makes 1½ cups.*

Serving Suggestion: Serve with roast beef, pork, lamb, tongue, or corned beef.

RAW APPLE CHUTNEY

2 medium apples, quartered and cored	1 tablespoon lemon juice
1 green pepper, seeded and cut up	¼ teaspoon salt
½ clove garlic	¼ teaspoon ground ginger
1 tablespoon sugar	⅛ teaspoon pepper
1 tablespoon vinegar	¾ teaspoon paprika
	½ cup seedless raisins

Put apples, green pepper, and garlic into blender container. Add cold water to cover. Cover; blend at medium speed until coarsely chopped. Drain thoroughly in colander; empty into bowl. Stir in remaining ingredients; mix well; chill. *Makes 2½ cups.*

ORANGE MARMALADE

4 large oranges
2 lemons
1½ cups water
⅛ teaspoon baking soda

5 cups sugar
1 package (1¾ ounces)
powdered pectin

Remove colored portion of rind from fruit with vegetable peeler. Put rinds and water into blender container. Cover; ▊ blend at medium speed until rinds are coarsely chopped. Empty into large saucepan; stir in baking soda. Heat to boiling; reduce heat; simmer 20 minutes. Remove and discard white membrane from oranges and lemons. Cut up oranges and lemons. Put half the fruit into blender container. Cover; ▊ blend at medium speed until chopped. Empty into saucepan with rinds. Repeat process with remaining fruit. Simmer 10 minutes. Add sugar and pectin. Bring to full rolling boil; boil, stirring constantly, 1 minute (accurate timing is important). Remove from heat; cool 10 minutes. Ladle into hot, sterilized jars. Seal at once. *Makes about 2½ pints*.

PEACH-ALMOND JAM

½ cup blanched almonds
About 3 pounds ripe
peaches
¼ cup lemon juice

7 cups sugar
½ bottle (3 ounces) liquid
pectin
½ teaspoon almond extract

Put almonds into blender container. Cover; ▊ blend at medium speed until chopped. Empty nuts into large saucepan. Wash peaches and cut into pieces; remove pits but do not peel. Put lemon juice and ½ cup peaches into blender container. Cover; blend at low speed until pureed. Add remaining peaches, about ½ cup at a time, blending until pureed (you should have 4½ cups puree). Add puree to almonds in saucepan. Stir in sugar. Bring to a full rolling boil, stirring frequently. Boil, stirring constantly, 1 minute (accurate timing is important). Remove from heat. Stir in pectin and almond extract immediately. Stir and skim for 5 minutes to cool slightly and to prevent fruit from floating. Ladle into hot, sterilized jars. Seal at once. Let stand two days before using. *Makes about 5 pints*.

NO-COOK STRAWBERRY JAM

1½ cups strawberries, washed
    and hulled
2 cups sugar

1 tablespoon lemon juice
3 tablespoons liquid pectin

If berries are large, cut in half. Put berries and sugar into blender container. Cover; blend at low speed until pureed. While blender is running, tip center cap and add lemon juice and pectin; blend until smooth. Ladle into jars; cover; refrigerate. Plan to use within three weeks. For longer storage, pour jam into freezer containers and freeze. *Makes 2½ cups*.

All jars for canning should be sterilized before they are used. Wash the jars and lids in hot, sudsy water; rinse thoroughly. Place them in a large kettle and cover them with water. Heat the water to boiling and then continue to boil for 10 minutes. Turn off the heat but leave the jars and lids in the water until you are ready to fill them. Then remove them with tongs and invert the jars on paper towels to drain. The jars should be both hot and dry when you fill them.

Calorie-Counters

The wise calorie-counter will reduce the quantities of all foods eaten and will avoid excess amounts of fat, sugar, and starch. But it is also important for a dieter to keep in mind that it is still necessary to maintain the proper balance of daily requirements from the basic four food groups (see page 30).

The low-calorie diet, like any other diet with a restricted choice of foods, tends to become monotonous. But the blender, by changing texture and facilitating new combinations, can make even the most limited range of foods attractive. The recipes that follow have been specially developed to give maximum satisfaction with a minimum number of calories. The trick is to think lower-calorie, cook lower-calorie, and eat lower-calorie.

COTTAGE CHEESE DIP
(13 calories per tablespoon)

1 cup creamed cottage
   cheese
2 teaspoons lemon juice
1 teaspoon Worcestershire
   sauce
1 vegetable bouillon cube

1 thin slice onion
3 radishes, cut in half
½ small green pepper,
   seeded and cut up
½ teaspoon celery seed

Put all ingredients into blender container in order listed. Cover; blend at medium speed until vegetables are chopped. If necessary, stop blender during processing and push ingredients toward blades with rubber spatula. Chill several hours. *Makes 1¼ cups.*

Weight-Watcher's Menu
Chicken Tarragon (page 229)
Steamed Spinach
Fresh Blueberries with Sweetened Mock Sour Cream (page 232)
Coffee

Opposite: Mock Sour Cream, page 232.

CLAM-TOMATO CONSOMME
(49 calories per serving

2 cups clam juice
1 medium tomato, cut up
½ small onion, cut up

1 thin slice lemon
½ teaspoon celery salt
Dash pepper

Put all ingredients into blender container in order listed. Cover; blend at high speed until smooth. Pour into saucepan; simmer 3 minutes. *Makes 3 servings.*

BOSTON CLAM CHOWDER
(76 calories per serving)

2 cans (7½ ounces each)
   minced clams
Water
1 medium onion, cut up
1 carrot, pared and cut up

¼ teaspoon salt
¼ teaspoon pepper
¼ teaspoon dried thyme
2 cups skim milk

228

Drain clams; measure clam liquid; add water to make 1 cup. Put clam-water mixture, onion, carrot, salt, pepper, and thyme into blender container. Cover; blend at medium speed just until vegetables are chopped. Pour into saucepan. Cover; cook over low heat about 20 minutes or until vegetables are tender. Add clams; stir in milk gradually. Simmer 5 minutes. *Makes 6 servings.*

DEVILED VEAL CUTLETS
(346 calories per serving)

1 pound veal cutlets
2 tablespoons all-purpose
   flour
¾ teaspoon salt
¼ teaspoon pepper
2 tablespoons butter or
   margarine
1 carrot, pared and cut up

1 stalk celery, cut up
1 medium onion, cut up
1½ cups water
2 teaspoons prepared
   horseradish
1 teaspoon prepared
   mustard
½ cup plain yogurt

Pound cutlets to ¼-inch thickness; cut into serving-size pieces. Dredge pieces in mixture of flour, salt, and pepper; reserve remaining flour mixture. Heat butter in large skillet; add veal and brown well on all sides. Put carrot, celery, onion, and water into blender container. Cover; ◼ blend at medium speed just until vegetables are chopped. Add to veal in skillet; cover; simmer 25 minutes. Put horseradish, mustard, yogurt, and reserved flour mixture into blender container. Cover; blend at high speed until smooth. Pour into skillet with veal. Cook, stirring constantly, until thickened. *Makes 4 servings.*

CHICKEN TARRAGON
(244 calories per serving)

1 medium onion, cut up	2 tablespoons butter or margarine
1 stalk celery, cut up	1 tablespoon all-purpose flour
1 small green pepper, seeded and cut up	1 teaspoon dried tarragon
1 clove garlic, halved	1 can (10¾ ounces) condensed chicken broth
2 chicken breasts, split	1 can (3 or 4 ounces) sliced mushrooms, drained
½ teaspoon salt	
⅛ teaspoon pepper	

Put onion, celery, green pepper, and garlic into blender container. Add water to cover. Cover; ◼ blend at medium speed just until vegetables are chopped. Drain thoroughly in colander; set aside. Sprinkle chicken with salt and pepper. Heat butter in large skillet. Add chicken; brown well on all sides; remove from pan. Add chopped vegetables to drippings left in pan; cook over medium heat, stirring occasionally, 5 minutes. Sprinkle with flour and tarragon; stir to blend. Stir in chicken broth and mushrooms; add chicken. Cover. Bring to a boil; reduce heat; simmer 30 to 35 minutes or until chicken is tender. *Makes 4 servings.*

FOIL-BAKED FISH
(249 calories per serving)

1 pound fish fillets
½ lemon, cut up
2 sprigs parsley
1 stalk celery, cut up
1 clove garlic, halved
2 tablespoons
    Worcestershire sauce

1 teaspoon salt
½ teaspoon dried basil
¼ teaspoon dried thyme
2 tablespoons softened
    butter or margarine

Heat oven to 400° F. Divide fish into four portions; place each on square of aluminum foil. Put remaining ingredients into blender container in order listed. Cover; blend at medium speed until lemon and celery are chopped. If necessary, stop blender during processing and push ingredients toward blades with rubber spatula. Top each portion of fish with one-fourth butter mixture. Wrap portions, using a double fold. Bake 30 minutes. *Makes 4 servings*.

SHRIMP JAMBALAYA
(203 calories per serving)

1 can (16 ounces) tomatoes
1 cup water
1 medium green pepper,
    seeded and cut up
2 stalks celery, cut up
1 medium onion, cut up
6 sprigs parsley

1 chicken bouillon cube
1¼ teaspoons salt
¾ teaspoon chili powder
½ cup regular rice
2 cups small to medium
    cooked, shelled shrimp

Put all ingredients except rice and shrimp into blender container in order listed. Cover; ⍁ blend at medium speed just until vegetables are chopped. Pour into saucepan; bring to a boil. Add rice; stir. Cover; simmer 20 to 25 minutes or until rice is tender. Add shrimp; heat 3 minutes. *Makes 4 servings*.

230

FLUFFY COTTAGE CHEESE OMELET
(128 calories per serving)

4 eggs, separated
3 tablespoons water
½ teaspoon salt
⅛ teaspoon pepper
½ cup creamed cottage
    cheese

1 thin slice onion
4 sprigs parsley
1 tablespoon butter or
    margarine

Heat oven to 325° F. Put egg yolks, water, salt, pepper, cottage cheese, onion, and parsley into blender container. Cover; blend at high speed until smooth. Beat egg whites in large bowl with electric mixer until stiff but not dry. Gently fold in egg yolk mixture. Heat butter in skillet with heatproof handle until bubbly but not browned. Add egg mixture. Cook over low heat 4 to 5 minutes or until omelet is puffy and underside is golden. Put skillet in oven. Bake 10 to 15 minutes or until omelet is dry and lightly browned on top. Loosen edges with spatula; slip gently onto warm serving plate. Serve immediately. *Makes 4 servings.*

231

JELLIED MEAT SALAD
(122 calories per serving with beef; 78 with poultry)

2 tablespoons cold water
1 tablespoon lemon juice
1 envelope unflavored
    gelatin
⅔ cup boiling water
2 beef or chicken bouillon
    cubes
1 stalk celery, cut up
1 small carrot, pared and
    cut up

¼ medium green pepper,
    seeded and cut up
1 thin slice onion
1 cup cubed cooked lean
    meat or poultry
1 cup cracked or crushed
    ice
Salad greens

Put cold water and lemon juice into blender container. Sprinkle on gelatin; let stand 1 minute.

Add boiling water and bouillon cubes. Cover; blend at low speed until gelatin and bouillon cubes are dissolved. Add remaining ingredients except salad greens to blender container in order listed. Cover; blend at medium speed just until vegetables and meat are chopped. If necessary, stop blender during processing and push ingredients toward blades with rubber spatula. Pour into 3-cup mold or four individual molds. Chill until set. Unmold onto salad greens. *Makes 4 servings.*

TOMATO-HERB SALAD DRESSING 🧂
(32 calories)

½ cup tomato juice
2 tablespoons vinegar
½ clove garlic
¼ small green pepper, seeded and cut up
6 sprigs parsley
¾ teaspoon Worcestershire sauce

½ teaspoon salt
¼ teaspoon dried basil
1 teaspoon sugar or equivalent amount of low-calorie sweetener
Dash pepper

Put all ingredients into blender container in order listed. Cover; blend at medium speed until vegetables are chopped. *Makes ¾ cups.*
Serving Suggestion: Serve with salad greens.

MOCK SOUR CREAM 🧂
(12 calories per tablespoon)

2 tablespoons skim milk
2 tablespoons lemon juice

1 cup creamed cottage cheese

Put all ingredients into blender container in order listed. Cover; blend at high speed until smooth. *Makes 1¼ cups.*
Serving Suggestions: Use as topping or as

ingredient in recipes in place of sour cream.
Dessert Topping: Prepare Mock Sour Cream.
Add low-calorie sweetener and vanilla to taste.

DIETER'S CHEESECAKE
(154 calories per serving with sugar; 109 with sweetener)

4 graham crackers
¼ teaspoon ground
  cinnamon
1½ cups skim milk
2 envelopes unflavored
  gelatin
¾ cup sugar or equivalent
  amount of low-calorie
  sweetener

2 eggs, separated
2 tablespoons lemon juice
1 thin slice orange
3 cups creamed cottage
  cheese
1 teaspoon vanilla
¼ teaspoon salt
¼ cup sugar

Break graham crackers into blender container.
Cover; blend at medium speed until crumbed.
Empty into bowl; stir in cinnamon. Sprinkle half the
crumb mixture over bottom of 8-inch springform
pan. Pour ½ cup milk into blender container.
Sprinkle on gelatin; let stand 1 minute. Heat
remaining 1 cup milk to boiling. Add to blender
container. Cover; blend at low speed until gelatin is
dissolved. Add ¾ cup sugar or equivalent amount of
low-calorie sweetener and egg yolks. Cover; blend at
high speed until smooth. Add remaining ingredients
except egg whites to blender container in order
listed. Cover; blend until smooth. If necessary, stop
blender during processing and push ingredients
toward blades with rubber spatula. Empty into large
bowl. Beat egg whites in second bowl with electric
mixer until foamy. Beat in ¼ cup sugar gradually.
Continue beating until stiff but not dry. Fold into
cheese mixture. Pour into prepared pan. Top with
remaining crumbs. Chill until set. *Makes 12
servings.*

233

Baby Foods

When you blender-prepare baby foods, you can cut the cost of feeding baby in half—and, perhaps even more important in a crowded kitchen, you can clear the shelves of many of those little jars and cans.

With a blender, you can also easily adjust your baby's diet to his changing needs. When the doctor recommends new foods be added, small amounts of that new food may be blended into combinations that your child already knows and likes. The new food may then be increased gradually until the recommended amount is accepted. When the time comes for junior foods, you can again make the transition by easy, delicious stages, mainly adding texture. When a child is finally ready to enjoy the full spread of the family table, the changeover can be achieved the same easy way—by a gradual process of adding ingredients and coarsening textures.

It is always a good idea to follow your doctor's recommendations for the foods to serve your baby. The recipes given here indicate relative quantities for good consistencies, but the ingredients can be varied to some extent. Cereal, of course, may be included in any fruit, vegetable, or meat puree.

MEAT FOR BABY

½ cup cubed cooked lean meat or poultry

4 to 6 tablespoons broth, milk, or formula
Salt (optional)

Put meat and liquid into blender container. Cover; blend at medium speed until perfectly smooth. Add salt to taste if desired. Heat to desired temperature. *Makes ½ cup.*

Note: Cubed cooked beef, lamb, pork, veal, chicken, or turkey may be used. Remove any skin, membrane, and fat from meat or poultry before cubing.

DINNER FOR BABY 🧂
(Using cooked foods)

½ cup cubed cooked lean
    meat or poultry
¼ cup cooked or canned
    vegetable (except corn),
    drained
¼ cup cooked rice,
    macaroni, or diced
    potato

½ cup vegetable cooking
    liquid, tomato juice,
    broth, milk, or formula
Salt (optional)

Put all ingredients except salt into blender container. Cover; blend at medium speed until perfectly smooth. Add salt to taste if desired. Heat before serving. *Makes about 1 cup.*

VEGETABLE FOR BABY 🧂

½ cup cooked or canned
    vegetable (except corn),
    drained

2 tablespoons vegetable
    cooking liquid or
    formula
Salt (optional)

Put vegetable and liquid into blender container. Cover; blend at low speed until perfectly smooth. Add salt to taste if desired. *Makes ½ cup.*

EGG FOR BABY

2 hard-cooked eggs, shelled
¼ cup milk

Salt (optional)

Start blender at medium speed. While blender is running, tip center cap and add eggs, one at a time, blending until chopped. Add milk; blend until perfectly smooth. Add salt to taste if desired. *Makes ½ cup.*

Egg for Junior: Reduce milk to 3 tablespoons. Proceed as for Egg for Baby blending to desired texture.

Consult your pediatrician before introducing new foods to baby. Use basic recipes in this chapter as a guide for amounts and blending times and then prepare your own combinations from family menus.

TODDLER CHICKEN SOUP

½ cup milk
2 tablespoons chicken broth
2 tablespoons cubed cooked chicken
2 tablespoons diced cooked carrots

1 teaspoon butter or margarine
1 teaspoon uncooked quick-cooking wheat cereal

Put all ingredients into blender container in order listed. Cover; blend at medium speed until chicken and carrots are finely chopped. Pour into saucepan. Cook 5 minutes, stirring constantly. *Makes about ¾ cup.*

JUNIOR MEAT DINNER

½ cup beef broth, tomato juice, or milk
½ cup raw diced lean beef or lamb
½ cup cut green beans, peas, diced carrots, or firmly packed spinach leaves

1 thin slice onion
½ cup cooked rice or pared, diced potato
Salt (optional)

Put all ingredients except salt into blender container in order listed. Cover; blend at medium speed until of desired texture. Pour into saucepan.
Cook, covered, over low heat 10 minutes, stirring occasionally, until meat is cooked. Add salt to taste if desired. *Makes about 1½ cups.*

Baby Meat Dinner: Prepare Junior Meat Dinner as above. Return cooked dinner to blender container. Cover; blend until perfectly smooth.

JUNIOR CHICKEN DINNER

⅔ cup chicken broth or milk
½ cup raw diced chicken or turkey, skin removed
½ cup pared, diced carrots

1 sprig parsley
½ cup cooked macaroni
Salt (optional)

Put all ingredients except salt into blender container in order listed. Cover; blend at medium speed until of desired texture. Pour into saucepan.
Cook, covered, over low heat 10 minutes, stirring occasionally, until chicken is cooked. Add salt to taste if desired. *Makes about 1½ cups.*

Baby Chicken Dinner: Prepare Junior Chicken Dinner as above. Return cooked dinner to blender container. Cover; blend until perfectly smooth.

237

FRUIT FOR BABY

¾ cup fresh or dried fruit
½ teaspoon sugar

2 teaspoons cooking liquid from fruit

If you are using fresh fruit, pare, pit or core it, and cut it up if needed. Put it into saucepan with small amount of water. Cover; simmer until tender. If you are using dried fruit, follow package directions for cooking. Then put fruit, sugar, and cooking liquid into blender container. Cover; blend at low speed until perfectly smooth. *Makes about ⅔ cup.*

FRUIT WITH CEREAL

1 cup canned peach slices, cut-up pears, or pitted plums, drained

2 tablespoons orange juice
¼ cup baby cereal

Put all ingredients into blender container in order listed. Cover; blend at high speed until smooth. *Makes about 1 cup.*

FRESH BANANA APPLESAUCE

2 to 3 tablespoons orange juice
1 to 2 teaspoons sugar

1 small ripe banana, cut up
1 small apple, pared, cored, and cut up

Put all ingredients into blender container in order listed. Cover; blend at high speed until smooth. *Makes about 1 cup.*

PEACH CUSTARD

½ cup canned peach slices or 2 large canned peach halves, drained

½ cup milk
1 egg
¼ teaspoon vanilla

Heat oven to 325° F. Put peaches and milk into blender container. Cover; blend at high speed until smooth. Add egg and vanilla. Cover; blend at low speed until smooth. Pour into two 5-ounce custard cups. Set in shallow pan. Pour water into pan to within 1 inch of top of custard. Bake 45 minutes to 1 hour or until knife inserted in center comes out clean. *Makes 2 servings.*

Index